Forever I Will Sing
Metered Guitar/Vocal Edition
Through-Composed Responsorial Psalms and Gospel Acclamations

November 27, 2022 – November 26, 2023
Year A

Music by Timothy R. Smith

Online Instructional Videos
Visit www.timothyrsmith.com for links to online instructional videos for each of the Responsorial Psalms and Gospel Acclamations. These are helpful in familiarizing cantors and instrumentalists with each piece.

Refrain Melodies for Assembly Worship Aids
To receive pdf of all refrain melodies at no additional charge, send copy of receipt to forever@timothyrsmith.com

Forever I Will Sing (Metered Guitar/Vocal Edition)
Through-Composed Responsorial Psalms and Gospel Acclamations
Year A – November 27, 2022 through November 26, 2023

Musical settings by Timothy R. Smith
This songbook © 2022, Timothy R. Smith. Published by TR TUNE, LLC. All rights reserved.
www.timothyrsmith.com
ISBN: 978-1-7350150-6-4

All musical settings by Timothy R. Smith. Some settings were previously published by OCP, 5536 NE Hassalo, Portland, OR 97213-3638; as indicated, they are available at www.ocp.org

Also available at www.timothyrsmith.com:
Forever I Will Sing 2023 Metered Keyboard Edition
Forever I Will Sing 2023 Classic Chant Edition

Publisher: TR TUNE, LLC, Waterford, MI   www.timothyrsmith.com
Composer: Timothy R. Smith
Editor: Barbara Bridge
Cover Art: Mary Dudek
             www.marydudekart.com

The Right Slash " / " in Gospel Acclamations indicates a pause or a breath at the end of the phrase before the slash.

We are still developing and refining this format and we welcome any feedback. Please feel free to contact me anytime if you have feedback about any aspect of this publication.
Tim Smith
tim@timothyrsmith.com

Singing the Psalm Settings

Psalm Refrains can be adapted to piano, organ, guitar accompaniment, or even SATB choir. The melodies, rhythms and harmonies are designed to embody the spirit of the text.

Verses are set for solo voice (Cantor) with keyboard or guitar accompaniment. The Guitar Edition features fewer page turns for easier use. The Classic Chant Edition features non-metered verses stacked with similar melodic contours. Refrains are uniform among all editions.

The mixed-meter settings of many of these Psalms were developed from extensive use of *Forever I Will Sing Classic Chant Edition* (still available for 2023). In the chant settings I became more aware of the natural rhythm of text. These settings are based on my perception of those natural rhythms.

Similar to how digital code is based on a series of *ones* and *zeros*, I believe rhythm of language can be based on syllable groupings of *twos* and *threes*, or *duples* and *triples*. In Example 1 consider the text in Psalm 105: *You descendants of Abraham, his servants.* I perceive the natural rhythm as this configuration of duples and triples:

Example 1

You de-scend-ants of A-bra-ham, his ser-vants,

In this instance, *descendants of* is a triple rhythm and the others are all duple. (eighth note = eighth note)

Consider in Example 2 this segment of Psalm 98:

Example 2

he has done won-drous deeds

Why not indicate the time signature changes?

While some of these Psalms fit within traditional time signatures, many of the settings in this book are driven by the duple/triple natural language rhythm. Since there is no recurring metric structure in this mixed meter environment, we feel indicating constantly changing time signatures would add unnecessary distraction. These rhythms are implemented by following the lowest value of the duple/triple rhythmic groupings – often the eighth note.

Of course, there are no absolutes. In Example 3, Psalm 116 (p. 84), the natural text rhythm inspires a specific novel rhythm in which the quarter note is the fundamental beat.

Also note the triplet rhythm (*3*) in which 3 eighth notes fill the duration of 2 eighth notes – This is the exception. Keep in mind that all eighth notes are equal (as in Examples 1 & 2), whether beamed in twos or threes *unless* there is a triplet (*3*) indicator as seen below:

Example 3

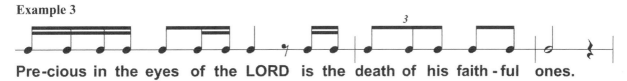

Pre-cious in the eyes of the LORD is the death of his faith - ful ones.

PAGE	REFRAIN	SUNDAY	PSALM REFERENCE
10	Let us go rejoicing	First Sunday of Advent	Psalm 122:1-2, 3-4, 4-5, 6-7, 8-9
14	Justice shall flourish in his time	Second Sunday of Advent	Psalm 72:1-2, 7-8, 12-13, 17
16	Sing to the Lord a new song	The Immaculate Conception of the Blessed Virgin Mary	Psalm 98:1, 2-3ab, 3cd-4
18	Lord, come and save us	Third Sunday of Advent	Psalm 146:6-7, 8-9, 9-10
20	You are the highest honor	Our Lady of Guadalupe	Judith 13:18bcde, 19
22	Let the Lord enter	Fourth Sunday of Advent	Psalm 24:1-2, 3-4, 5-6
24	Forever I will sing	The Nativity of The Lord (Christmas): Vigil Mass	Psalm 89:4-5, 16-17, 27, 29
26	Today is born our savior	The Nativity of The Lord (Christmas): During the Night	Psalm 96:1-2, 2-3, 11-12, 13
28	A light will shine on us this day	The Nativity of The Lord (Christmas): At Dawn	Psalm 97:1, 6, 11-12
30	All the ends of the earth	The Nativity of The Lord (Christmas): During The Day	Psalm 98:1, 2-3, 3-4, 5-6
32	Blessed are those who fear the Lord	The Holy Family of Jesus, Mary and Joseph	Psalm 128:1-2, 3, 4-5
34	May God bless us in his mercy	Solemnity of Mary the Holy Mother of God	Psalm 67: 2-3, 5, 6, 8
36	Lord every nation on earth	The Epiphany of the Lord	Psalm 72:1-2, 7-8, 10-11, 12-13
38	Here am I, Lord; I come to do your will	Second Sunday in Ordinary Time	Psalm 40:2, 4, 7-8, 8-9, 10
40	The Lord is my light and my salvation	Third Sunday in Ordinary Time	Psalm 27:1, 4, 13-14
42	Blessed are the poor in spirit	Fourth Sunday in Ordinary Time	Psalm 146:6-7, 8-9, 9-10
44	The just man is a light	Fifth Sunday in Ordinary Time	Psalm 112:4-5, 6-7, 8-9
46	Blessed are they who follow the law	Sixth Sunday in Ordinary Time	Psalm 119:1-2, 4-5, 17-18, 33-34
48	The Lord is kind and merciful	Seventh Sunday in Ordinary Time	Psalm 103:1-2, 3-4, 8, 10, 12-13
50	Be merciful, O Lord,	Ash Wednesday	Psalm 51:3-4, 5-6ab, 12-13, 14 & 17
52	Be merciful, O Lord,	First Sunday of Lent	Psalm 51:3-4, 5-6ab, 12-13, 14 & 17
54	Lord, let your mercy be on us	Second Sunday of Lent	Psalm 33:4-5, 18-19, 20, 22
56	If today you hear his voice	Third Sunday of Lent	Psalm 95:1-2, 6-7, 8-9
58	The Lord is my shepherd	Fourth Sunday of Lent	Psalm 23:1-3a, 3b-4, 5, 6
60	With the Lord there is mercy	Fifth Sunday of Lent	Psalm 130:1-2, 3-4, 5-6, 7-8
62	My God, my God,	Psalm Sunday of the Passion of the Lord	Psalm 22:8-9, 17-18, 19-20, 23-24
64	Our blessing cup	Thursday of the Lord's Supper: (Holy Thursday) At the Evening Mass	Psalm 116:12-13, 15-16bc, 17-18
66	Father, into your hands I commend	Friday of the Passion of the Lord (Good Friday)	Psalm 31:2, 6, 12-13, 15-16, 17, 25
68	Lord, send out your Spirit	The Easter Vigil in the Holy Night	Psalm 104:1-2, 5-6, 10, 12, 13-14, 24, 35
70	The earth is full	The Easter Vigil in the Holy Night	Psalm 33:4-5, 6-7, 12-13, 20 & 22
72	You are my inheritance	The Easter Vigil in the Holy Night	Psalm 16:5, 8, 9-10, 11
74	Let us sing to the Lord	The Easter Vigil in the Holy Night	Exodus 15:1-2, 3-4, 5-6, 17-18
76	I will praise you, Lord	The Easter Vigil in the Holy Night	Psalm 30:2, 4, 5-6, 11-12, 13
78	You will draw water	The Easter Vigil in the Holy Night	Isaiah 12:2-3, 4bcd, 5-6
80	Lord, you have the words	The Easter Vigil in the Holy Night	Psalm 19:8, 9, 10, 11
82	Like a deer	The Easter Vigil in the Holy Night	Psalm 42:3, 5; 43:3, 4
84	You will draw water	The Easter Vigil in the Holy Night	Isaiah 12:2-3, 4bcd, 5-6
86	Create a clean heart	The Easter Vigil in the Holy Night	Psalm 51:12-13, 14-15, 18-19
88	Alleluia, alleluia, alleluia	The Easter Vigil Gospel Acclamation	Psalm 118:1-2, 16-17, 22-23
90	This is the day	Easter Sunday: Mass during the Day	Psalm 118:1-2, 16-17, 22-23
92	Give thanks to the Lord	Second Sunday of Easter (or Sunday of Divine Mercy)	Psalm 118:2-4, 13-15, 22-24
96	Lord, you will show us the path to life	Third Sunday of Easter	Psalm 16:1-2, 5, 7-8, 9-10, 11
98	The Lord is my shepherd	Fourth Sunday of Easter	Psalm 23:1-3a, 3b-4, 5, 6
100	Lord, let your mercy be on us	Fifth Sunday of Easter	Psalm 33:1-2, 4-5, 18-19

PAGE	REFRAIN	SUNDAY	PSALM REFERENCE
102	Let all the earth cry out to God with joy	Sixth Sunday of Easter	Psalm 66:1-3, 4-5, 6-7, 16, 20
104	God mounts his throne	The Ascension of the Lord	Psalm 47:2-3, 6-7, 8-9
106	I believe that I shall see	Seventh Sunday of Easter	Psalm 27:1, 4, 7-8
108	Blessed the people the Lord has chosen	Pentecost Sunday: Extended Vigil Mass	Psalm 33:10-11, 12-13, 14-15
110	Glory and praise forever	Pentecost Sunday: Extended Vigil Mass	Daniel 3:52, 53, 54, 55, 56
112	Lord, you have the words	Pentecost Sunday: Extended Vigil Mass	Psalm 19:8, 9, 10, 11
114	Give thanks to the Lord	Pentecost Sunday: Extended Vigil Mass	Psalm 107:2-3, 4-5, 6-7, 8-9
116	Lord, send out your Spirit	Pentecost Sunday: Extended Vigil Mass	Psalm 104:1-2, 24 & 35, 27-28, 29, 30
118	Lord, send out your Spirit	Pentecost Sunday: At the Mass during the Day	Psalm 104:1, 24, 29-30, 31, 34
120	Glory and praise forever	The Most Holy Trinity	Daniel 3:52, 53, 54, 55
122	Praise the Lord, Jerusalem	The Most Holy Body and Blood of Christ (Corpus Christi)	Psalm 147:12-13, 14-15, 19-20
124	We are his people	11th Sunday in Ordinary Time	Psalm 100:1-2, 3, 5
126	Lord, in your great love	12th Sunday in Ordinary Time	Psalm 69:8-10, 14, 17, 33-35
128	Forever I will sing	13th Sunday in Ordinary Time	Psalm 89:2-3, 16-17, 18-19
130	I will praise your name forever	14th Sunday in Ordinary Time	Psalm 145:1-2, 8-9, 10-11, 13-14
132	The seed that falls on good ground	15th Sunday in Ordinary Time	Psalm 65:10, 11, 12-13, 14
134	Lord, you are good and forgiving	16th Sunday in Ordinary Time	Psalm 86:5-6, 9-10, 15-16
136	Lord, I love your commands	17th Sunday in Ordinary Time	Psalm 119:57, 72, 76-77, 127-128, 129-130
138	The Lord is king	The Transfiguration of the Lord	Psalm 97:1-2, 5-6, 9
140	Lord, let us see your kindness	19th Sunday in Ordinary Time	Psalm 85:9, 10, 11-12, 13-14
142	Lord, go up to your place of rest	The Assumption of the Blessed Virgin Mary: Vigil Mass	Psalm 132:6-7, 9-10, 13-14
144	The queen stands	The Assumption of the Blessed Virgin Mary: during the Day	Psalm 45:10, 11, 12, 16
146	O God, let all the nations	20th Sunday in Ordinary Time	Psalm 67:2-3, 5, 6, 8
148	Lord, your love is eternal	21st Sunday in Ordinary Time	Psalm 138:1-2, 2-3, 6, 8
150	My soul is thirsting for you	22nd Sunday in Ordinary Time	Psalm 63:2, 3-4, 5-6, 8-9
152	If today you hear his voice	23rd Sunday in Ordinary Time	Psalm 95:1-2, 6-7, 8-9
154	The Lord is kind and merciful	24th Sunday in Ordinary Time	Psalm 103:1-2, 3-4, 9-10, 11-12
156	The Lord is near to all who call	25th Sunday in Ordinary Time	Psalm 145:2-3, 8-9, 17-18
158	Remember your mercies	26th Sunday in Ordinary Time	Psalm 25:4-5, 6-7, 8-9
160	The vineyard of the Lord	27th Sunday in Ordinary Time	Psalm 80:9, 12, 13-14, 15-16, 19-20
162	I shall live in the house of the Lord	28th Sunday in Ordinary Time	Psalm 23:1-3a, 3b-4, 5, 6
164	Give the Lord glory and honor	29th Sunday in Ordinary Time	Psalm 96:1, 3, 4-5, 7-8, 9-10
166	I love you, Lord, my strength.	30th Sunday in Ordinary Time	Psalm 18:2-3, 3-4, 47, 51
168	Lord, this is the people	All Saints	Psalm 24:1bc-2, 3-4ab, 5-6
170	In you, Lord	31st Sunday in Ordinary Time	Psalm 131:1, 2, 3
172	My soul is thirsting for you	32nd Sunday in Ordinary Time	Psalm 63:2, 3-4, 5-6, 7-8
174	Blessed are those who fear the Lord	33rd Sunday in Ordinary Time	Psalm 128:1-2, 3, 4-5
176	Blessed be the name of the Lord	Thanksgiving Day	Psalm 113:1-2, 3-4, 5-6, 7-8
178	The Lord is my shepherd	Our Lord Jesus Christ, King of the Universe	Psalm 23:1-2, 2-3, 5-6
180	Blessed the people	Rite of Entrance into the Order of Catechumens	Psalm 33:4-5, 12-13, 18-19, 20 & 22
182	Blessed are those who fear the Lord	Selected Psalm for Weddings	Psalm 128:1-2, 3, 4-5
184	The Lord is kind and merciful	Selected Psalm for Funerals	Psalm 103:8 & 10, 13-14, 15-16, 17-18
186	The Lord is my light and my salvation	Selected Common (Seasonal) Psalm for Ordinary Time	Psalm 27:1, 4, 13-14

Scripture Index

PAGE	PSALM REFERENCE
120	Daniel 3:52, 53, 54, 55
110	Daniel 3:52, 53, 54, 55, 56
74	Exodus 15:1-2, 3-4, 5-6, 17-18
78	Isaiah 12:2-3, 4bcd, 5-6
84	Isaiah 12:2-3, 4bcd, 5-6
20	Judith 13:18bcde, 19
96	Psalm 16:1-2, 5, 7-8, 9-10, 11
72	Psalm 16:5, 8, 9-10, 11
166	Psalm 18:2-3, 3-4, 47, 51
80	Psalm 19:8, 9, 10, 11
112	Psalm 19:8, 9, 10, 11
62	Psalm 22:8-9, 17-18, 19-20, 23-24
178	Psalm 23:1-2, 2-3, 5-6
58	Psalm 23:1-3a, 3b-4, 5, 6
98	Psalm 23:1-3a, 3b-4, 5, 6
162	Psalm 23:1-3a, 3b-4, 5, 6
22	Psalm 24:1-2, 3-4, 5-6
168	Psalm 24:1bc-2, 3-4ab, 5-6
158	Psalm 25:4-5, 6-7, 8-9
40	Psalm 27:1, 4, 13-14
186	Psalm 27:1, 4, 13-14
106	Psalm 27:1, 4, 7-8
76	Psalm 30:2, 4, 5-6, 11-12, 13
66	Psalm 31:2, 6, 12-13, 15-16, 17, 25
100	Psalm 33:1-2, 4-5, 18-19
108	Psalm 33:10-11, 12-13, 14-15
180	Psalm 33:4-5, 12-13, 18-19, 20 & 22
54	Psalm 33:4-5, 18-19, 20, 22
70	Psalm 33:4-5, 6-7, 12-13, 20 & 22
38	Psalm 40:2, 4, 7-8, 8-9, 10
82	Psalm 42:3, 5; 43:3, 4
144	Psalm 45:10, 11, 12, 16
104	Psalm 47:2-3, 6-7, 8-9
86	Psalm 51:12-13, 14-15, 18-19
50	Psalm 51:3-4, 5-6ab, 12-13, 14 & 17
52	Psalm 51:3-4, 5-6ab, 12-13, 14 & 17
172	Psalm 63:2, 3-4, 5-6, 7-8
150	Psalm 63:2, 3-4, 5-6, 8-9
132	Psalm 65:10, 11, 12-13, 14
102	Psalm 66:1-3, 4-5, 6-7, 16, 20
34	Psalm 67: 2-3, 5, 6, 8
146	Psalm 67:2-3, 5, 6, 8
126	Psalm 69:8-10, 14, 17, 33-35
36	Psalm 72:1-2, 7-8, 10-11, 12-13

Page	SCRIPTURE REFERENCE
14	Psalm 72:1-2, 7-8, 12-13, 17
160	Psalm 80:9, 12, 13-14, 15-16, 19-20
140	Psalm 85:9, 10, 11-12, 13-14
134	Psalm 86:5-6, 9-10, 15-16
128	Psalm 89:2-3, 16-17, 18-19
24	Psalm 89:4-5, 16-17, 27, 29
56	Psalm 95:1-2, 6-7, 8-9
152	Psalm 95:1-2, 6-7, 8-9
26	Psalm 96:1-2, 2-3, 11-12, 13
164	Psalm 96:1, 3, 4-5, 7-8, 9-10
138	Psalm 97:1-2, 5-6, 9
28	Psalm 97:1, 6, 11-12
30	Psalm 98:1, 2-3, 3-4, 5-6
16	Psalm 98:1, 2-3ab, 3cd-4
124	Psalm 100:1-2, 3, 5
48	Psalm 103:1-2, 3-4, 8, 10, 12-13
154	Psalm 103:1-2, 3-4, 9-10, 11-12
184	Psalm 103:8 & 10, 13-14, 15-16, 17-18
116	Psalm 104:1-2, 24 & 35, 27-28, 29, 30
68	Psalm 104:1-2, 5-6, 10, 12, 13-14, 24, 35
118	Psalm 104:1, 24, 29-30, 31, 34
114	Psalm 107:2-3, 4-5, 6-7, 8-9
44	Psalm 112:4-5, 6-7, 8-9
176	Psalm 113:1-2, 3-4, 5-6, 7-8
64	Psalm 116:12-13, 15-16bc, 17-18
88	Psalm 118:1-2, 16-17, 22-23
90	Psalm 118:1-2, 16-17, 22-23
92	Psalm 118:2-4, 13-15, 22-24
46	Psalm 119:1-2, 4-5, 17-18, 33-34
136	Psalm 119:57, 72, 76-77, 127-128, 129-130
10	Psalm 122:1-2, 3-4, 4-5, 6-7, 8-9
32	Psalm 128:1-2, 3, 4-5
174	Psalm 128:1-2, 3, 4-5
182	Psalm 128:1-2, 3, 4-5
60	Psalm 130:1-2, 3-4, 5-6, 7-8
170	Psalm 131:1, 2, 3
142	Psalm 132:6-7, 9-10, 13-14
148	Psalm 138:1-2, 2-3, 6, 8
130	Psalm 145:1-2, 8-9, 10-11, 13-14
156	Psalm 145:2-3, 8-9, 17-18
18	Psalm 146:6-7, 8-9, 9-10
42	Psalm 146:6-7, 8-9, 9-10
122	Psalm 147:12-13, 14-15, 19-20

Responsorial Psalm Refrain Alphabetical Index

PAGE	REFRAIN	PAGE	REFRAIN
28	A light will shine on us this day	54	Lord, let your mercy be on us
30	All the ends of the earth	100	Lord, let your mercy be on us
88	Alleluia, alleluia, alleluia	68	Lord, send out your Spirit
50	Be merciful, O Lord,	116	Lord, send out your Spirit
52	Be merciful, O Lord,	118	Lord, send out your Spirit
42	Blessed are the poor in spirit	168	Lord, this is the people
46	Blessed are they who follow the law	134	Lord, you are good and forgiving
32	Blessed are those who fear the Lord	80	Lord, you have the words
174	Blessed are those who fear the Lord	112	Lord, you have the words
182	Blessed are those who fear the Lord	96	Lord, you will show us the path to life
176	Blessed be the name of the Lord	148	Lord, your love is eternal
180	Blessed the people	34	May God bless us in his mercy
108	Blessed the people the Lord has chosen	62	My God, my God,
86	Create a clean heart	150	My soul is thirsting for you
66	Father, into your hands I commend	172	My soul is thirsting for you
24	Forever I will sing	146	O God, let all the nations
128	Forever I will sing	64	Our blessing cup
92	Give thanks to the Lord	122	Praise the Lord, Jerusalem
114	Give thanks to the Lord	158	Remember your mercies
164	Give the Lord glory and honor	16	Sing to the Lord a new song
110	Glory and praise forever	70	The earth is full
120	Glory and praise forever	44	The just man is a light
104	God mounts his throne	48	The Lord is kind and merciful
38	Here am I, Lord; I come to do your will	154	The Lord is kind and merciful
106	I believe that I shall see	184	The Lord is kind and merciful
166	I love you, Lord, my strength.	138	The Lord is king
162	I shall live in the house of the Lord	40	The Lord is my light and my salvation
76	I will praise you, Lord	186	The Lord is my light and my salvation
130	I will praise your name forever	58	The Lord is my shepherd
56	If today you hear his voice	98	The Lord is my shepherd
152	If today you hear his voice	178	The Lord is my shepherd
170	In you, Lord	156	The Lord is near to all who call
14	Justice shall flourish in his time	144	The queen stands
102	Let all the earth cry out to God with joy	132	The seed that falls on good ground
22	Let the Lord enter	160	The vineyard of the Lord
10	Let us go rejoicing	90	This is the day
74	Let us sing to the Lord	26	Today is born our savior
82	Like a deer	124	We are his people
36	Lord every nation on earth	60	With the Lord there is mercy
18	Lord, come and save us	72	You are my inheritance
142	Lord, go up to your place of rest	20	You are the highest honor
136	Lord, I love your commands	78	You will draw water
126	Lord, in your great love	84	You will draw water
140	Lord, let us see your kindness		

Four-Part Harmonizations of Gospel Acclamations

Below are the Gospel Acclamations used throughout this book in four-part harmony. They may be useful for singers or instrumentalists.

Acclamation: (Keyboard/SATB) NO. I

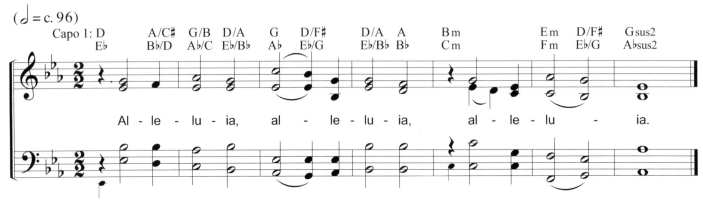

Acclamation: (Keyboard/SATB) NO. II

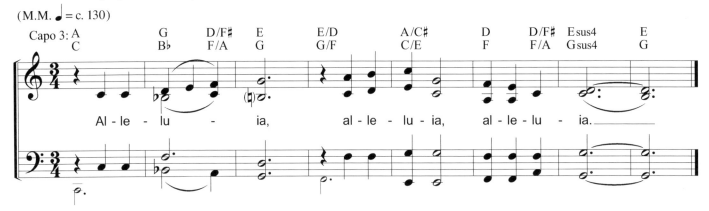

Acclamation: (Keyboard/SATB) NO. III

Acclamation: (Keyboard/SATB) NO. IV

(M.M. ♩ = c. 116)

Al-le-lu - ia,___ al-le-lu - ia,___ al-le-lu - ia.

Acclamation: (Keyboard/SATB) NO. V

(M.M. ♪ = c. 150)

Al - le -lu - ia, al-le-lu-ia. Al - le-lu - ia, al - le-lu - ia.

Acclamation: (Keyboard/SATB) NO. VI

(M.M. ♩ = c. 104)

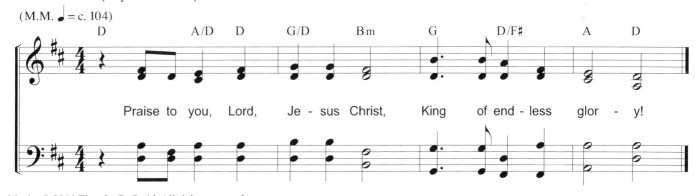

Praise to you, Lord, Je - sus Christ, King of end - less glor - y!

Acclamation: (Keyboard/SATB) NO. VII

(♩ = c. 90)

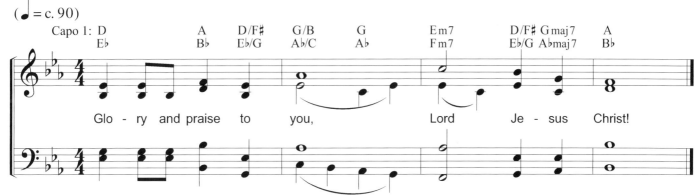

Glo - ry and praise to you, Lord Je - sus Christ!

9

First Sunday of Advent

November 27

Psalm 122:1-2, 3-4, 4-5, 6-7, 8-9

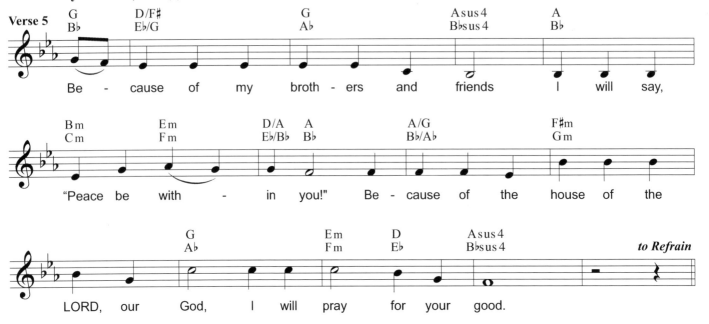

Verse 5

G   D/F#   G   Asus4   A
Bb   Eb/G   Ab   Bbsus4   Bb

Be - cause of my broth - ers and friends I will say,

Bm   Em   D/A A   A/G   F#m
Cm   Fm   Eb/Bb Bb Bb/Ab Gm

"Peace be with - in you!" Be - cause of the house of the

G   Em   D   Asus4   *to Refrain*
Ab   Fm   Eb   Bbsus4

LORD, our God, I will pray for your good.

Gospel Acclamation: cf. Psalm 85:8

Acclamation: (Keyboard/SATB) NO. III

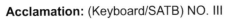

(M.M. ♩ = c. 160)

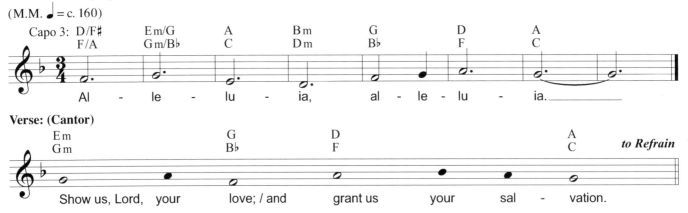

Capo 3: D/F#   Em/G   A   Bm   G   D   A
        F/A   Gm/Bb   C   Dm   Bb   F   C

Al - le - lu - ia, al - le - lu - ia.____

Verse: (Cantor)

Em   G   D   A   *to Refrain*
Gm   Bb   F   C

Show us, Lord, your love; / and grant us your sal - vation.

Second Sunday of Advent

December 4

Psalm 72:1-2, 7-8, 12-13, 17

Verse 3

For he shall res-cue the poor when he cries out, and the af-

flict-ed when he has no one to help him. He shall have pit-y for the

low-ly and the poor; the lives of the poor he shall save.___

Verse 4

May his name be blessed for-ev-er; as long as the sun his

name shall re-main. In him shall all the tribes of the earth be

blessed; all the na-tions shall pro-claim his hap-pi-ness.

Gospel Acclamation: Luke 3:4, 6

Acclamation: (Keyboard/SATB) NO. I

Al-le-lu-ia, al-le-lu-ia, al-le-lu-ia.

Verse: (Cantor)

Prepare the way of the Lord, / make straight his paths: / all flesh shall see the salva-tion of God.

Music: *Mass of the Sacred Heart*; Timothy R. Smith, © 2007, 2010, Timothy R. Smith. Published by OCP. All rights reserved.

The Immaculate Conception of the Blessed Virgin Mary

December 8

Psalm 98:1, 2-3ab, 3cd-4

Verse 3

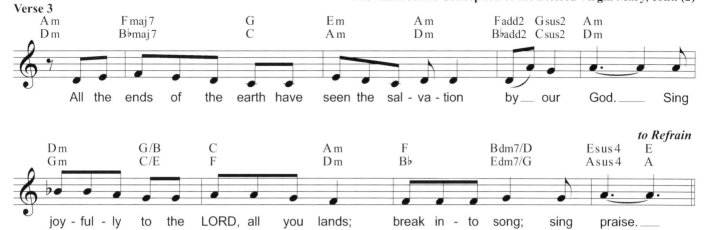

All the ends of the earth have seen the sal-va-tion by our God. Sing

to Refrain

joy-ful-ly to the LORD, all you lands; break in-to song; sing praise.

Gospel Acclamation: Luke 1:28

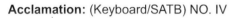

Acclamation: (Keyboard/SATB) NO. IV

(M.M. ♩ = c. 116)

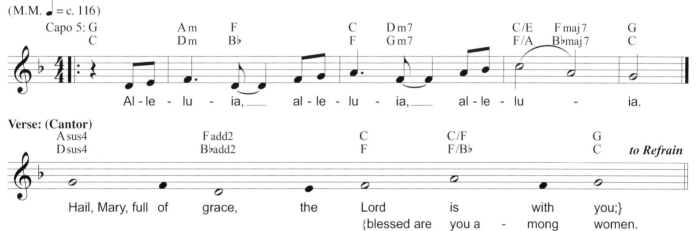

Al-le-lu - ia,— al-le-lu - ia,— al-le-lu - ia.

Verse: (Cantor)

Hail, Mary, full of grace, the Lord is with you;}
{blessed are you a - mong women.

Music © 2014, Timothy R. Smith. Published by TR TUNE, LLC. All rights reserved.

17

Third Sunday of Advent

December 11

Psalm 146:6-7, 8-9, 9-10

Verse 3

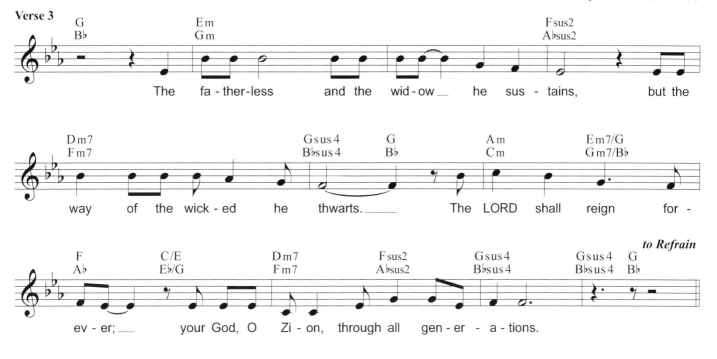

The fa-ther-less and the wid-ow___ he sus-tains, but the

way of the wick-ed he thwarts.___ The LORD shall reign for-

to Refrain

ev-er;___ your God, O Zi-on, through all gen-er-a-tions.

Gospel Acclamation: Isaiah 61:1 (cited in Luke 4:18)

Acclamation: (Keyboard/SATB) NO. IV

(M.M. ♩ = c. 116)

Al-le-lu-ia,___ al-le-lu-ia,___ al-le-lu - ia. ia.

Verse: (Cantor)

to Refrain

The Spirit of the LORD is up-on me, / because he has a-nointed me to bring glad tidings to the poor.

Our Lady of Guadalupe

December 12

*"Sunday, December 12 is the Third Sunday of Advent, and the Feast of Our Lady of Guadalupe is omitted this year.
Our Lady of Guadalupe may be appropriately honored in the Homily, Universal Prayer, and hymns during the
Sunday liturgy. If pastoral advantage calls for it (cf. GIRM, no. 376), a Votive Mass of Our Lady of Guadalupe
may be celebrated on a weekday before or after December 12, with the proper readings and prayers."*

United States Conference of Catholic Bishops Committee on Divine Worship

Judith 13:18bcde, 19

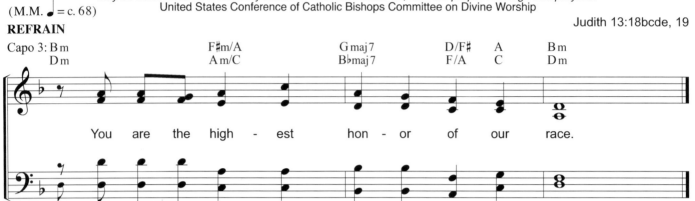

REFRAIN

You are the high-est hon-or of our race.

Verse 1

Bless-ed are you, daugh-ter, by the Most High God, a-bove all the wom-en on

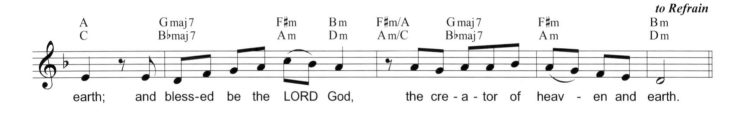

earth; and bless-ed be the LORD God, the cre-a-tor of heav-en and earth.

to Refrain

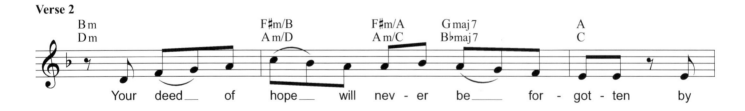

Verse 2

Your deed of hope will nev-er be for-got-ten by

to Refrain

those who tell of the might of God. You are the high-est hon-or of our race.

Gospel Acclamation:

Acclamation: (Keyboard/SATB) NO. II

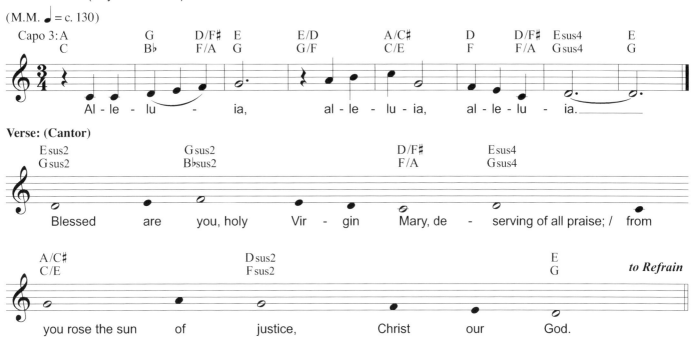

Al - le - lu - ia, al - le - lu - ia, al - le - lu - ia.

Verse: (Cantor)

Blessed are you, holy Vir - gin Mary, de - serving of all praise; / from you rose the sun of justice, Christ our God.

to Refrain

Music © 2014, Timothy R. Smith. Published by TR TUNE, LLC. All rights reserved.

Fourth Sunday of Advent
December 18

Psalm 24:1-2, 3-4, 5-6

ho-ly place? One whose hands are sin-less, whose heart is clean, who de-

sires not what is vain. _____

Verse 3

He shall re-ceive a bless-ing from the LORD, a re-ward from God his

sav-ior. Such is the race that seeks for him, that seeks___ the

face of the God___ of Ja-cob. _____

Gospel Acclamation: Matthew 1:23

Acclamation: (Keyboard/SATB) NO. I

Al - le - lu - ia, al - le - lu - ia, al - le - lu - ia.

Verse: (Cantor)

The virgin shall conceive and bear a son, and they shall name him Em-man - u - el.

The Nativity of The Lord (Christmas): At the Vigil Mass

December 24

(M.M. ♩ = c. 90)

Psalm 89:4-5, 16-17, 27, 29

REFRAIN

For ev - er I____ will sing the good - ness of____ the Lord. For

ev - er I will sing____ the good - ness of____ the Lord.

Verse 1 (M.M. ♩ = c. 76)

I have made a cov - e - nant with my cho - sen one, I have sworn to Da - vid my

ser - vant: for - ev - er will I con - firm your pos - ter - i - ty

to Refrain

and es - tab - lish your throne for all gen - er - a - tions.

Verse 2 (M.M. ♩ = c. 76)

Bless - ed the peo - ple who know the joy - ful shout; in the light of your

coun - te - nance, O LORD; they walk. At your name they re - joice all the day,

to Refrain

and through your jus - tice they are ex - alt - ed.

Verse 3 (M.M. ♩ = c. 76)

He shall say of me, "You are my fa - ther, my God, the rock, my

sav - ior." For - ev - er I will main - tain my kind - ness toward

to Refrain

him, and my cov - e - nant with him stands firm.

Gospel Acclamation:

Acclamation: (Keyboard/SATB) NO. V

(M.M. ♪ = c. 150)

Al - le - lu - ia, al - le - lu - ia. Al - le - lu - ia, al - le - lu - ia.

Verse: (Cantor)

to Refrain

Tomorrow the wickedness of the earth will be de - stroyed:/ the Savior of the world reign ov - er us.

The Nativity of the Lord (Christmas):
At the Mass during the Night

December 25

Psalm 96:1-2, 2-3, 11-12, 13

Verse 3

Let the heav-ens be glad and the earth re - joice; let the sea and what fills it re - sound;_____ let the plains be joy-ful and all that is in them! Then shall all the trees of the for - est ex - ult._____

Verse 4

They shall ex - ult be - fore____ the LORD, for he comes; for he comes to rule the earth._____ He shall rule the world with jus - tice and the peo - ples with his con - stan - cy._____

to Refrain

Gospel Acclamation: Luke 2:10-11

Acclamation: (Keyboard/SATB) NO. V

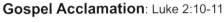

(M.M. ♪ = c. 150)

Al - le - lu - ia, al - le - lu - ia. Al - le - lu - ia, al - le - lu - ia.

Verse: (Cantor)   *to Refrain*

I proclaim to you good news of great joy: / to - day a Sav - ior is born for us, / Christ the Lord.

The Nativity of the Lord (Christmas):
At the Mass at Dawn

(M.M. ♩ = c. 63)

December 25

Psalm 97:1, 6, 11-12

Gospel Acclamation: Luke 2:14
Acclamation: (Keyboard/SATB) NO. V

Al - le -lu - ia, al - le -lu - ia. Al - le -lu - ia, al - le - lu - ia.

Verse: (Cantor) *to Refrain*

Glory to God___ in the highest, / and on earth peace to those on whom his fav - or rests.

The Nativity of the Lord (Christmas):
At the Mass during the Day

December 25

Psalm 98:1, 2-3, 3-4, 5-6

REFRAIN

All the ends of the earth have seen the sav - ing power of God.

Verse 1 (M.M. ♩ = c. 71)

Sing to the LORD a new song, for he has done won - drous deeds; his right hand has won vic - t'ry for him, his ho - ly arm. *to Refrain*

Verse 2 (M.M. ♩ = c. 71)

The LORD has made his sal - va - tion known: in the sight of the na - tions he has re - vealed his jus - tice. He has re - mem - bered his kind - ness and his faith - ful - ness toward the house of Is - ra - el. *to Refrain*

Verse 3 (M.M. ♩ = c. 71)

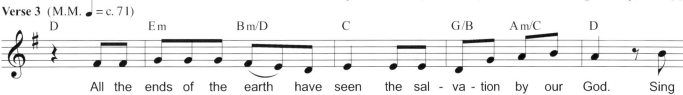

All the ends of the earth have seen the sal - va - tion by our God. Sing

joy - ful - ly to the LORD, all you lands; break in - to song; sing praise.

to Refrain

Verse 4 (M.M. ♩ = c. 71)

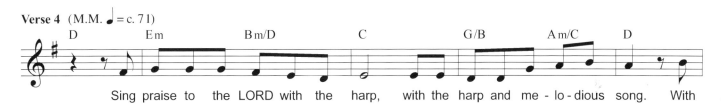

Sing praise to the LORD with the harp, with the harp and me - lo - dious song. With

to Refrain

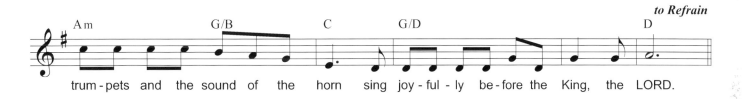

trum - pets and the sound of the horn sing joy - ful - ly be - fore the King, the LORD.

Gospel Acclamation:

Acclamation: (Keyboard/SATB) NO. V

(M.M. ♪ = c. 150)

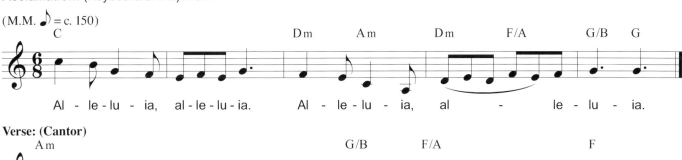

Al - le - lu - ia, al - le - lu - ia. Al - le - lu - ia, al - le - lu - ia.

Verse: (Cantor)

A hol - y day has dawned up - on us. Come, you na - tions, and a -

to Refrain

dore the Lord. / For to - day a great light has come up - on the earth.

The Holy Family of Jesus, Mary and Joseph

December 30

Psalm 128:1-2, 3, 4-5, 6

bless you from ___ Zi - on: ___ may you see the pros - per - i - ty

of Je - ru - sa - lem all the days ___ of your life.

Gospel Acclamation: Colossians 3:15a, 16a

Acclamation: (Keyboard/SATB) NO. I

Al - le - lu - ia, al - le - lu - ia, al - le - lu - ia.

Verse: (Cantor) *to Refrain*

Let the peace of Christ con -trol your hearts; / let the word of Christ dwell in you richly.

Solemnity of Mary, the Holy Mother of God

January 1

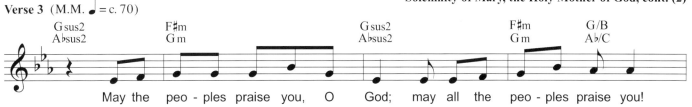

Verse 3 (M.M. ♩ = c. 70)

May the peo-ples praise you, O God; may all the peo-ples praise you!

May God bless us, and may all the ends of the earth fear him!

Gospel Acclamation: Hebrews 1:1-2

Acclamation: (Keyboard/SATB) NO. I

(♩ = c. 96)

Al - le - lu - ia, al - le - lu - ia, al - le - lu - ia.

Verse: (Cantor)

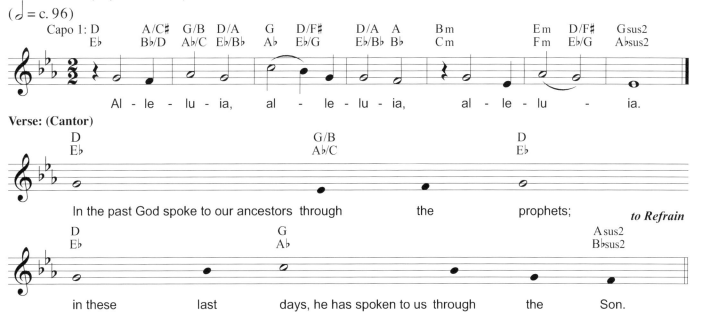

In the past God spoke to our ancestors through the prophets;

in these last days, he has spoken to us through the Son.

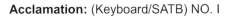

The Epiphany of the Lord

January 8

Psalm 72:1-2, 7-8, 10-11, 12-13

Verse 4

For he shall res-cue the poor when he cries out, and the af-flict-ed when he has no one to help him. He shall have pit-y for the low-ly and the poor; the lives of the poor he shall save.

to Refrain

Gospel Acclamation: Matthew 2:2

Acclamation: (Keyboard/SATB) NO. II

(M.M. ♩ = c. 130)

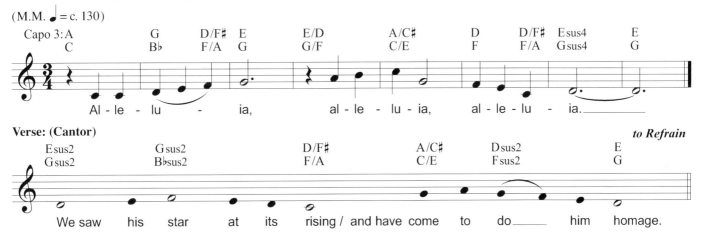

Al-le-lu - ia, al-le-lu-ia, al-le-lu - ia.

Verse: (Cantor)   *to Refrain*

We saw his star at its rising / and have come to do him homage.

Music © 2014, Timothy R. Smith. Published by TR TUNE, LLC. All rights reserved.

Second Sunday in Ordinary Time

January 15

Psalm 40:2, 4, 7-8, 8-9, 10

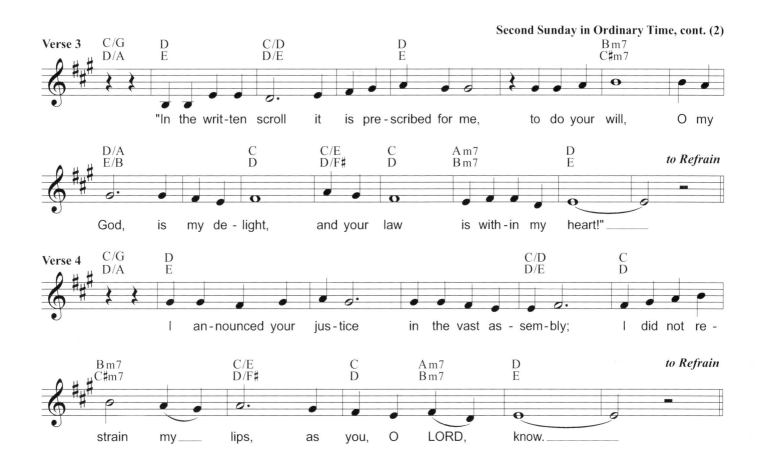

Verse 3
"In the writ-ten scroll it is pre-scribed for me, to do your will, O my God, is my de-light, and your law is with-in my heart!" _____ *to Refrain*

Verse 4
I an-nounced your jus-tice in the vast as-sem-bly; I did not re-strain my ___ lips, as you, O LORD, know. _____ *to Refrain*

Gospel Acclamation: John 1:14a, 12a

Acclamation: (Keyboard/SATB) NO. IV

(M.M. ♩ = c. 116)

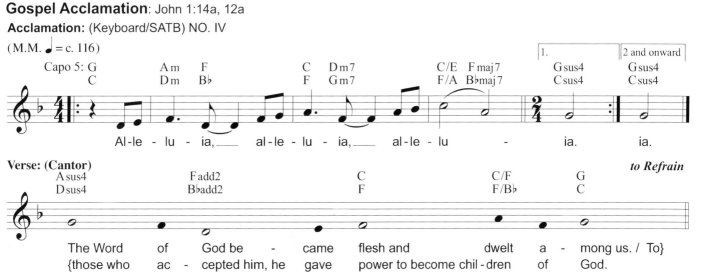

Al-le-lu-ia,___ al-le-lu-ia,___ al-le-lu - ia. ia.

Verse: (Cantor)   *to Refrain*

The Word of God be - came flesh and dwelt a - mong us. / To}
{those who ac-cepted him, he gave power to become chil-dren of God.

Third Sunday in Ordinary Time

January 22

Psalm 27:1, 4, 13-14

life, that I may gaze on the love-li-ness____ of the
LORD, and con-tem-plate his tem-ple.

Verse 3

I be-lieve that I shall see the boun-ty of the LORD in the
land of the liv-ing. Wait for the LORD with cour-age;____
____ be stout-heart-ed, and wait for the LORD.

Gospel Acclamation: cf. Matthew 4:23

Acclamation: (Keyboard/SATB) NO. I

Al-le-lu-ia, al-le-lu-ia, al-le-lu-ia.

Verse: (Cantor) *to Refrain*

Jesus proclaimed the Gospel of the kingdom and cured every dis-ease a-mong the people.

Fourth Sunday in Ordinary Time

January 29

Verse 3

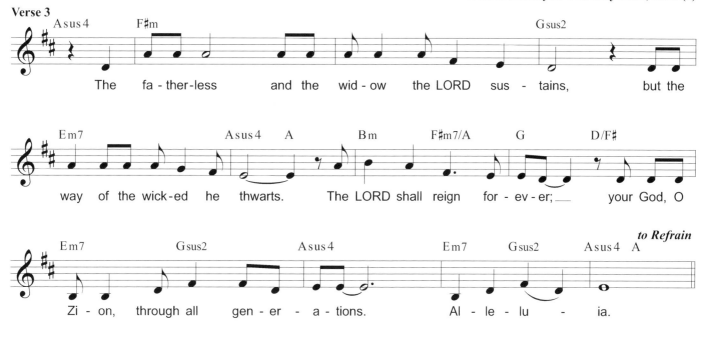

The fa-ther-less and the wid-ow the LORD sus - tains, but the way of the wick-ed he thwarts. The LORD shall reign for - ev - er; ___ your God, O Zi - on, through all gen - er - a - tions. Al - le - lu - ia.

Gospel Acclamation: Matthew 5:12a

Acclamation: (Keyboard/SATB) NO. I

($\quad$ = c. 96)

Al - le - lu - ia, al - le - lu - ia, al - le - lu - ia.

Verse: (Cantor)

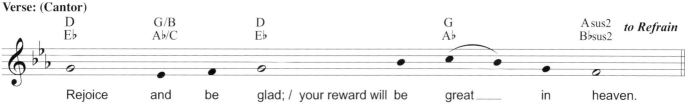

Rejoice and be glad; / your reward will be great ___ in heaven.

Fifth Sunday in Ordinary Time

February 5

Psalm 112:4-5, 6-7, 8-9

Verse 3

His heart is stead - fast; he shall not fear. Lav - ish - ly he

gives to the poor; his jus - tice shall en - dure___ for -

to Refrain

ev - er; his horn shall be ex - alt - ed in glo - ry.

Gospel Acclamation: John 8:12
Acclamation: (Keyboard/SATB) NO. III

(M.M. ♩ = c. 160)

Al - le - lu - ia, al - le - lu - ia.___

Verse: (Cantor)

to Refrain

I am the light of the world, says the Lord;}
{whoever fol - lows me will have the light of life.

Sixth Sunday in Ordinary Time

February 12

Psalm 119:1-2, 4-5, 17-18, 33-34

Verse 3
Be good to your ser-vant, that I may live and keep your words. O-pen my eyes, that I may con-sid-er the won-ders of your law.

to Refrain

Verse 4
In-struct me, O LORD, in the way of your stat-utes, that I may ex-act-ly ob-serve them. Give me dis-cern-ment, that I may ob-serve your law and keep it with all my heart.

to Refrain

Gospel Acclamation: cf. Matthew 11:25
Acclamation: (Keyboard/SATB) NO. II

(M.M. ♩ = c. 130)

Al-le-lu - ia, al-le-lu-ia, al-le-lu - ia.

Verse: (Cantor)
Blessed are you, Fath-er, Lord of heav - en and earth; / you have re-vealed to little ones the mysteries of the kingdom.

to Refrain

Seventh Sunday in Ordinary Time

February 19

Psalm 103:1-2, 3-4, 8, 10, 12-13

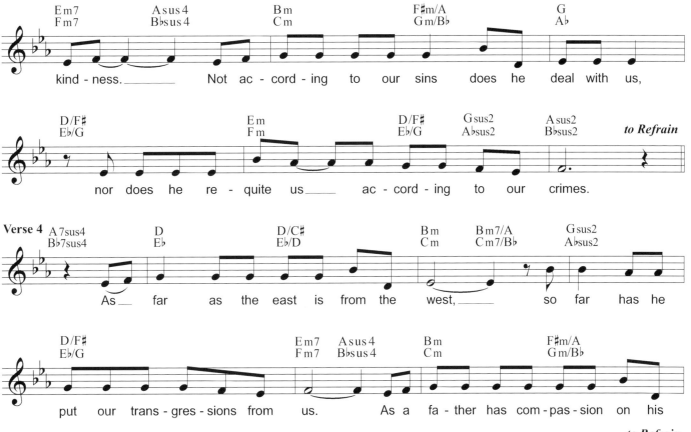

Gospel Acclamation: 1 John 2:5

Acclamation: (Keyboard/SATB) NO. I

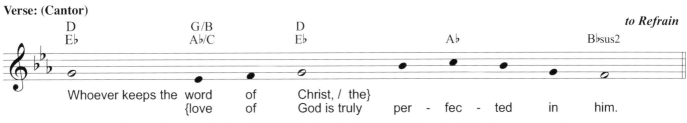

Verse: (Cantor)

Ash Wednesday

February 22

Psalm 51:3-4, 5-6ab, 12-13, 14 & 17

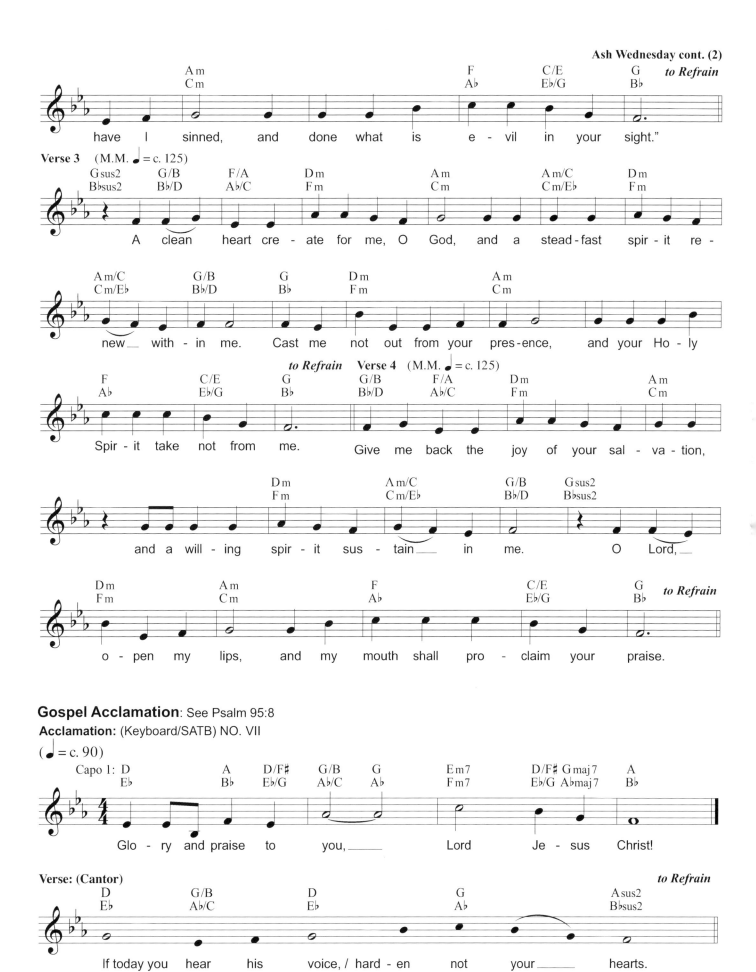

Gospel Acclamation: See Psalm 95:8

Acclamation: (Keyboard/SATB) NO. VII

Verse: (Cantor)

First Sunday of Lent

February 26

Psalm 51:3-4, 5-6ab, 12-13, 14 & 17

have I sinned, and done what is e - vil in your sight."

Verse 3 (M.M. ♩ = c. 125)

A clean heart cre - ate for me, O God, and a stead - fast spir - it re -

new __ with - in me. Cast me not out from your pres - ence, and your Ho - ly

to Refrain **Verse 4** (M.M. ♩ = c. 125)

Spir - it take not from me. Give me back the joy of your sal - va - tion,

and a will - ing spir - it sus - tain __ in me. O Lord, __

to Refrain

o - pen my lips, and my mouth shall pro - claim your praise.

Gospel Acclamation: Matthew 4:4b

Acclamation: (Keyboard/SATB) NO. VI

(M.M. ♩ = c. 104)

Praise to you, Lord, Je - sus Christ, King of end - less glor - y!

Verse: (Cantor) *to Refrain*

One does not live on bread a - lone, / but on every word that comes forth from the mouth of God.

Second Sunday of Lent
March 5

Psalm 33:4–5, 18–19, 20, 22

up-on those who hope for his kind — ness, to de - liv - er them from

death and pre - serve them in spite of fam - ine.

to Refrain

Verse 3

Our soul __ waits for the LORD, who is our help and our

shield. __ May your kind - ness, O LORD, be up -

to Refrain

on us __ who have put __ our hope in __ you. __

Gospel Acclamation: Matthew 17:5

Acclamation: (Keyboard/SATB) NO. VII

(♩ = c. 90)

Glo - ry and praise to you, Lord Je - sus Christ!

Verse: (Cantor)

to Refrain

From the shining cloud the Father's voice is heard: / This is my belov - ed Son, hear him.

Third Sunday of Lent

March 12

Psalm 95:1-2, 6-7, 8-9

Verse 3

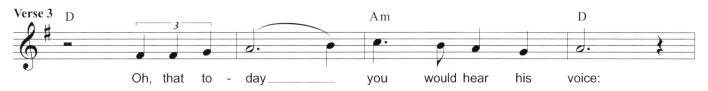

Oh, that to - day _____ you would hear his voice:

"Hard - en not your hearts as at Mer - i - bah, as in the day of Mas - sah __ in the

des - ert, __ where your fath - ers __ tempt - ed me; they test - ed me __ though

to Refrain

they had __ seen __ my __ works." __

Gospel Acclamation: cf. John 4:42, 15

Acclamation: (Keyboard/SATB) NO. VI

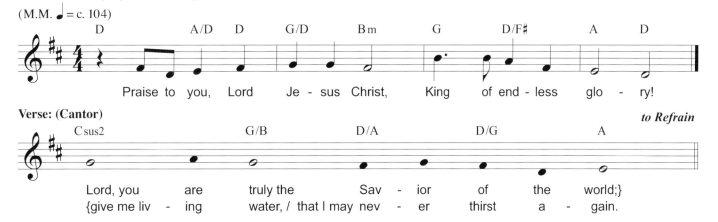

Praise to you, Lord Je - sus Christ, King of end - less glo - ry!

Verse: (Cantor)   *to Refrain*

Lord, you are truly the Sav - ior of the world;}
{give me liv - ing water, / that I may nev - er thirst a - gain.

Fourth Sunday of Lent

March 19

Psalm 23:1-3a, 3b-4, 5, 6

Verse 3

F / Ab G/F / Bb/Ab Em / Gm

You spread the ta - ble be - fore me in the sight of my

Am / Cm F / Ab G / Bb A/E / C/G

foes; you a - noint my head with oil;___

C/G / Eb/Bb F / Ab Gsus4 / Bbsus4 G / Bb *to Refrain*

___ my cup___ o - ver - flows.

Verse 4

F / Ab G/F / Bb/Ab Em / Gm

On - ly good - ness and kind - ness fol - low me all the days of my

Am / Cm F / Ab G / Bb A/E / C/G

life; and I shall dwell in the house of the LORD___

to Refrain

C/G / Eb/Bb F / Ab Gsus4 / Bbsus4 G / Bb

___ for years___ to___ come.

Gospel Acclamation: John 8:12

Acclamation: (Keyboard/SATB) NO. VI

(M.M. ♩ = c. 104)

D A/D D G/D Bm G D/F# A D

Praise to you, Lord Je - sus Christ, King of end - less glo - ry!

Verse: (Cantor) *to Refrain*

Csus2 G/B D/A D/G A

I am the light of the world, says the Lord; / whoever follows me will have the light of life.

Fifth Sunday of Lent
March 26

Psalm 130:1-2, 3-4, 5-6, 7-8

(M.M. ♩ = c. 80)

REFRAIN

With the Lord there is mer-cy and full-ness of _____ re-demp-tion.

(Keyboard)

Verse 1

Out of the depths I cry to you, O LORD;

LORD, hear my voice! Let your ears be at-ten-tive to my

voice in sup - pli - ca - tion. _____

to Refrain

Verse 2

If you, O LORD, mark in - iq - ui - ties, LORD, who can stand?

But with you is for-give-ness, that you may be__ re - vered. _____

to Refrain

Verse 3

I trust in the LORD; my soul trusts in his word. More than

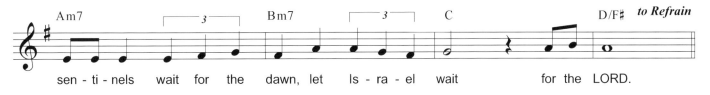

sen - ti - nels wait for the dawn, let Is - ra - el wait for the LORD.

Verse 4

For with the LORD is kind - ness and with him

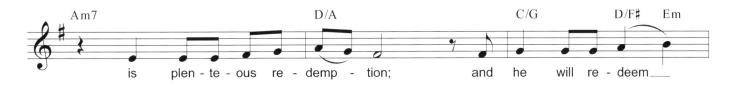

is plen - te - ous re - demp - tion; and he will re - deem

Is - ra - el from all their in - i - qui - ties.

Gospel Acclamation: John 11:25a, 26

Acclamation: (Keyboard/SATB) NO. VI

(M.M. ♩ = c. 104)

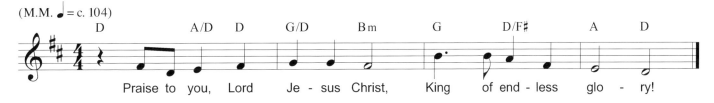

Praise to you, Lord Je - sus Christ, King of end - less glo - ry!

Verse: (Cantor) *to Refrain*

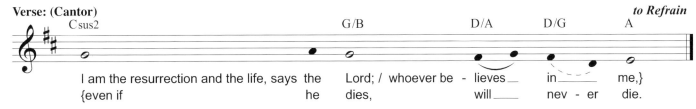

I am the resurrection and the life, says the Lord; / whoever be - lieves in me,}
{even if he dies, will nev - er die.

Palm Sunday of the Passion of the Lord

(M.M. ♩ = c. 89)

April 2

Psalm 22:8-9, 17-18, 19-20, 23-24

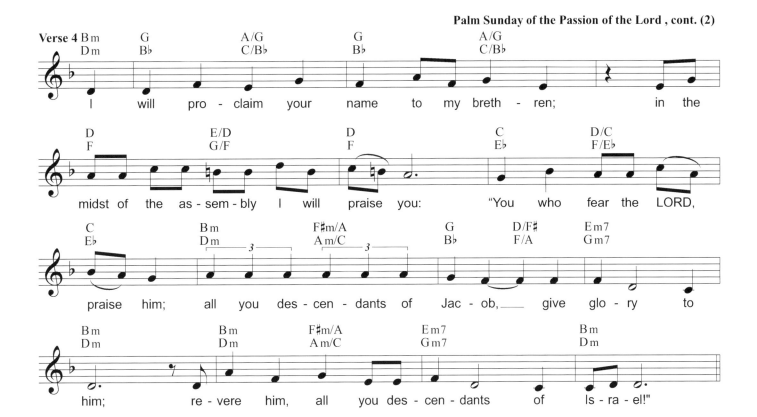

Verse 4

I will pro-claim your name to my breth-ren; in the midst of the as-sem-bly I will praise you: "You who fear the LORD, praise him; all you des-cen-dants of Jac-ob,___ give glo-ry to him; re-vere him, all you des-cen-dants of Is-ra-el!"

Gospel Acclamation: Philippians 2:8-9
Acclamation: (Keyboard/SATB) NO. VII

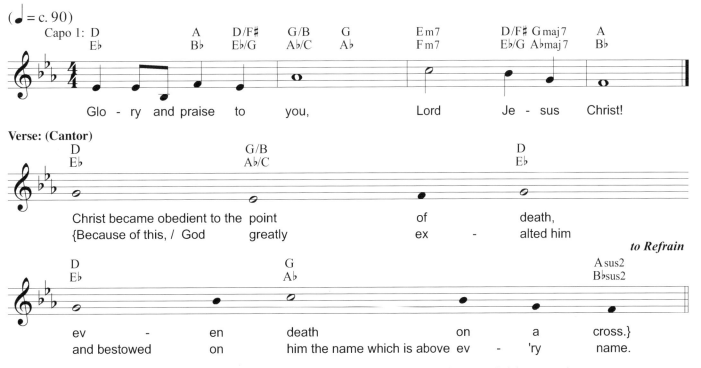

(♩ = c. 90)

Glo-ry and praise to you, Lord Je-sus Christ!

Verse: (Cantor)

Christ became obedient to the point of death,
{Because of this, / God greatly ex - alted him

to Refrain

ev - en death on a cross.}
and bestowed on him the name which is above ev - 'ry name.

Thursday of the Lord's Supper (Holy Thursday):
At the Evening Mass

April 6

Psalm 116:12-13,15-16bc, 17-18

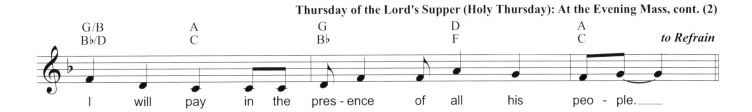

I will pay in the pres-ence of all his peo-ple.

to Refrain

Gospel Acclamation: John 13:34

Acclamation: (Keyboard/SATB) NO. VII

Glo-ry and praise to you, Lord Je-sus Christ!

Verse: (Cantor)

to Refrain

I give you a new commandment, says the Lord: / love one an-other as I have loved you.

Friday of the Passion of the Lord (Good Friday)

(M.M. ♩ = c. 120)   *April 7*   Psalm 31:2, 6, 12-13, 15-16, 17, 25

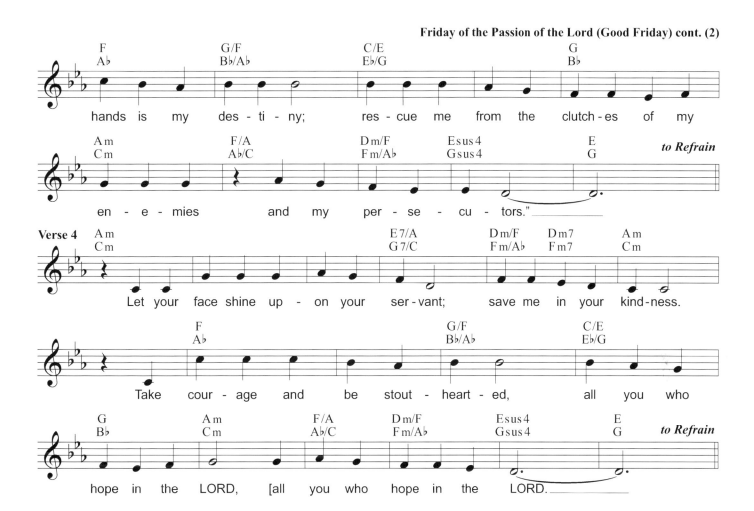

hands is my des-ti-ny; res-cue me from the clutch-es of my

to Refrain

en-e-mies and my per-se-cu-tors."

Verse 4

Let your face shine up-on your ser-vant; save me in your kind-ness.

Take cour-age and be stout-heart-ed, all you who

to Refrain

hope in the LORD, [all you who hope in the LORD.

Gospel Acclamation: Philippians 2:8-9

Acclamation: (Keyboard/SATB) NO. VII

(♩ = c. 90)

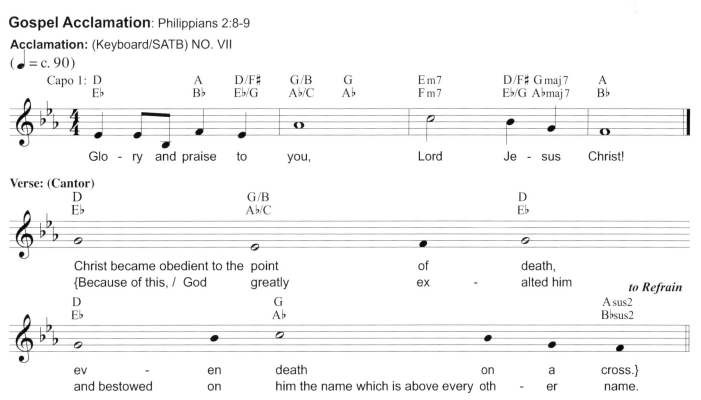

Glo-ry and praise to you, Lord Je-sus Christ!

Verse: (Cantor)

Christ became obedient to the point of death,
{Because of this, / God greatly ex - alted him

to Refrain

ev - en death on a cross.}
and bestowed on him the name which is above every oth - er name.

The Easter Vigil in the Holy Night

Responsorial Psalm (following first reading) *April 8*

(M.M. ♩ = c. 116)

Psalm 104:1-2, 5-6, 10, 12, 13-14, 24, 35

The Easter Vigil in the Holy Night, cont. (3)
Alternate Responsorial Psalm (following first reading)

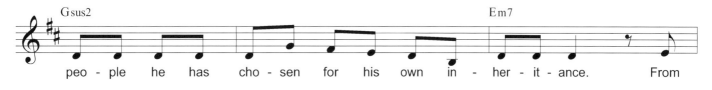

people he has cho-sen for his own in - her - it - ance. From

heav-en the LORD looks down; he sees___ all___ man - kind.

Verse 4

Our soul waits for the LORD, who is___ our help and our shield. May your

kind-ness, O LORD, be up - on us___ who have put our hope in you.

The Easter Vigil in the Holy Night, cont. (5)
Responsorial Psalm (following second reading)

Psalm 16:5, 8, 9-10, 11

(M.M. ♩ = c. 106)

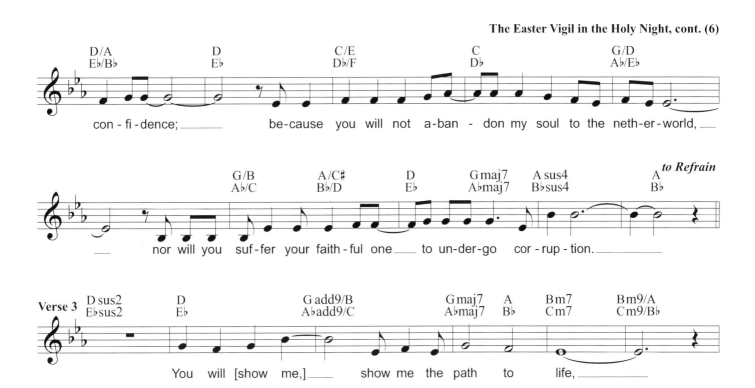

con - fi -dence; _____ be-cause you will not a-ban - don my soul to the neth-er-world, _____

_____ nor will you suf-fer your faith-ful one _____ to un-der-go cor - rup - tion. _____

Verse 3

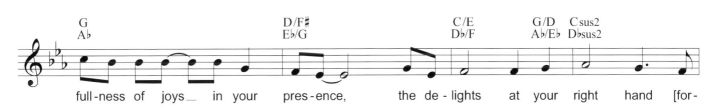

You will [show me,] _____ show me the path to life, _____

full -ness of joys ___ in your pres -ence, the de - lights at your right hand [for-

ev - er,] _____ for - ev - er.

to Refrain

73

Responsorial Psalm (following third reading)

(M.M. ♩ = c. 92)

Exodus 15:1-2, 3-4, 5-6, 17-18

Responsorial Psalm (following fourth reading)

(M.M. ♩ = c. 118)

Psalm 30:2, 4, 5-6, 11-12, 13

mo - ment; a life - time, his good will. At night - fall, weep - ing en - ters

to Refrain

in, but with the dawn,_____ re - joic - ing.

Verse 3

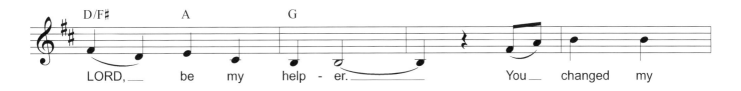

Hear, O LORD, and have pit - y [have pit - y] on me; O

LORD,___ be my help - er._____ You___ changed my

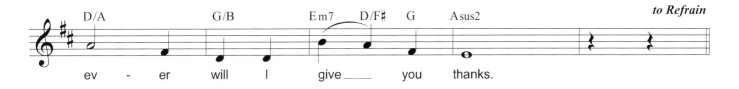

mourn - ing in - to danc - ing; O LORD,___ my God, for -

to Refrain

ev - er will I give____ you thanks.

77

The Easter Vigil in the Holy Night, cont. (11)
Responsorial Psalm (following fifth reading)
Isaiah 12:2-3, 4bcd, 5-6

to Refrain

alt - ed _____ is his name. _____

Verse 3

Sing praise to the LORD for his glo - rious a - chieve - ment; let this be

known through-out all the earth. Shout with ex - ul - ta - tion, O cit - y of Zi - on, for

to Refrain

great in your midst is the Ho - ly One of Is - ra - el! _____

Responsorial Psalm (following sixth reading)

(M.M. ♩ = c. 124)

Psalm 19:8, 9, 10, 11

Lord, you have the words, Lord, you have the words, you have the words of ev-er-last-ing life. *(Keyboard)*

Verse 1
The law of the LORD is per-fect, re-fresh-ing the soul;___ the de-
cree of the LORD is trust-wor-thy,___ giv-ing wis-dom to the sim-ple.___ *to Refrain*

Verse 2
The pre-cepts of the LORD are right,___ re-joic-ing the heart;___ the com-
mand of the LORD is clear,___ en-light-en-ing the eye. *to Refrain*

Verse 3
The fear of the LORD is pure,___ en-dur-ing for-ev-er;___ the

to Refrain

or - di - nanc - es ___ of the LORD are true, all of them just.

Verse 4

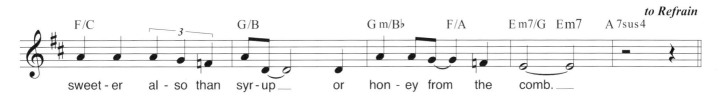

They are more pre - cious than gold, than a heap of pur - est gold; ___

to Refrain

sweet - er al - so than syr - up ___ or hon - ey from the comb. ___

Option A, when Baptism is celebrated
Responsorial Psalm (following seventh reading)

Psalm 42:3, 5; 43:3, 4

(M.M. ♩ = c. 64)
REFRAIN

Capo 3: A/E
C/G

Like a deer that longs for run-ning streams, my soul__ longs for you, my

God, my soul__ longs for you, my God.

Verse 1

A-thirst is my soul for God,__ the liv-ing God. When shall I

go__ and be-hold__ the face__ of God?

to Refrain

Verse 2

I went with the throng__ and led them in pro-ces-sion__

to the house of__ God, a-mid loud cries of joy__ and thanks-

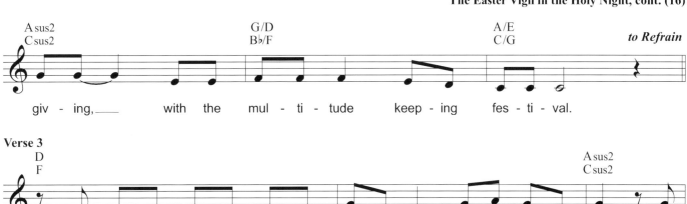

giv - ing, ___ with the mul - ti - tude keep - ing fes - ti - val.

Verse 3

Send forth your light and your fi - del - i - ty; they shall lead me on and

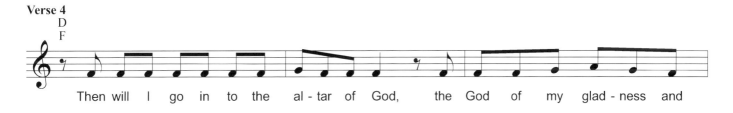

bring me to your ho - ly moun - tain, ___ to your dwell - ing-place.

Verse 4

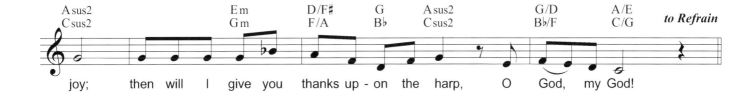

Then will I go in to the al - tar of God, the God of my glad - ness and

joy; then will I give you thanks up - on the harp, O God, my God!

The Easter Vigil in the Holy Night, cont. (17)

Responsorial Psalm (following seventh reading)
Or: Option B, when Baptism is not celebrated

(M.M. ♩ = c. 120)

Isaiah 12:2-3, 4bcd, 5-6

to Refrain

alt - ed _____ is his name. _____

Verse 3

Sing praise to the LORD for his glo - rious a -

chieve - ment; let this be known through-out all the earth. Shout with ex - ul -

ta - tion, O cit - y of Zi - on, ___ for great in your midst is the

to Refrain

Ho - ly One of Is - ra - el! _____

The Easter Vigil in the Holy Night, cont. (19)

Or: Option C, when Baptism is not celebrated
Responsorial Psalm (following seventh reading)

Psalm 51:12-13, 14-15, 18-19

(M.M. ♩= c. 77)
REFRAIN

Cre - ate _____ a clean heart, a clean heart in me, O God.

Verse 1 (M.M. ♩= c. 69)

A clean heart cre - ate for me, O God, and a stead - fast

spir - it re - new _____ with - in me. _____ Cast me not out from your

to Refrain

pres - ence, and your Ho - ly Spir - it take not from me.

Verse 2 (M.M. ♩= c. 69)

Give me back the joy of your sal - va - tion, and a will - ing

spir - it sus - tain _____ in me. I will teach trans - gres - sors your

to Refrain

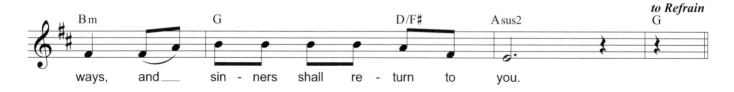

ways, and _____ sin - ners shall re - turn to you.

Verse 3 (M.M. ♩ = c. 69)

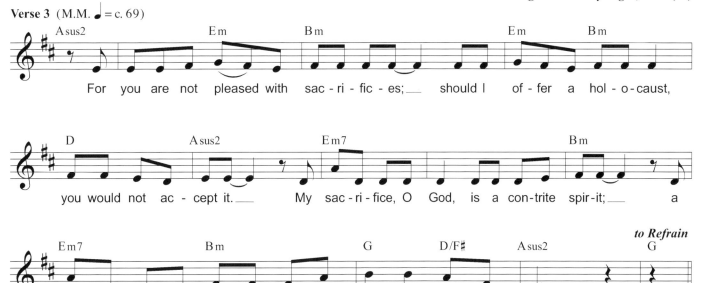

For you are not pleased with sac-ri-fic-es; ___ should I of-fer a hol-o-caust,

you would not ac-cept it. ___ My sac-ri-fice, O God, is a con-trite spir-it; ___ a

to Refrain

heart con-trite and hum-bled, ___ O God, you will not spurn.

Responsorial Psalm: Psalm 118:1-2, 16-17, 22-23

Acclamation: (Keyboard/SATB) NO. II

Verse 3

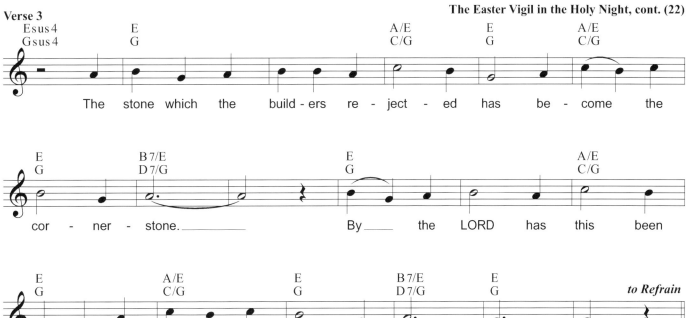

The stone which the build-ers re-ject-ed has be-come the

cor-ner-stone._____ By____ the LORD has this been

done; it is won-der-ful in our eyes._____

to Refrain

Easter Sunday of the Resurrection of the Lord:
At the Mass during the Day

(M.M. ♩ = c. 156)

REFRAIN [or: Alleluia]

April 9

Psalm 118:1-2, 16-17, 22-23

This is the day the Lord has made; let us re-joice and be glad.

Verse 1

Give thanks to the LORD, for he is good, for his mer-cy en-dures for-ev-er. Let the house of Is-ra-el say, "His mer-cy en-dures for-ev-er."

to Refrain

Verse 2

"The right hand of the LORD has struck with pow'r; the right hand of the LORD is ex-alt-ed. I shall not die, but live, and de-clare the works of the LORD."

to Refrain

Verse 3

The stone which the build-ers re-ject-ed has be-come the cor-ner-stone. By the LORD has this been done; it is won-der-ful in our eyes.

to Refrain

Gospel Acclamation: cf. 1 Corinthians 5:7b-8a

Acclamation: (Keyboard/SATB) NO. V

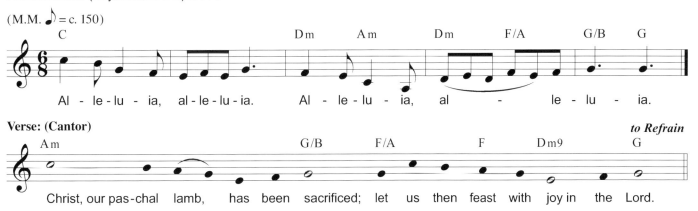

Al-le-lu-ia, al-le-lu-ia. Al-le-lu-ia, al-le-lu-ia.

Verse: (Cantor)

to Refrain

Christ, our pas-chal lamb, has been sacrificed; let us then feast with joy in the Lord.

Second Sunday of Easter (or Sunday of Divine Mercy)

April 16

(M.M. ♩ = c. 114)

REFRAIN [or: Alleluia]

Psalm 118:2-4, 13-15, 22-24

Gospel Acclamation: John 20:29
Acclamation: (Keyboard/SATB) NO. III

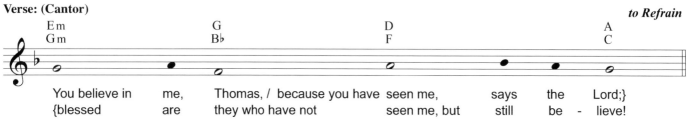

Al - le - lu - ia, al - le - lu - ia.

Verse: (Cantor)   *to Refrain*

You believe in me, Thomas, / because you have seen me, says the Lord;}
{blessed are they who have not seen me, but still be - lieve!

Third Sunday of Easter

April 23

Psalm 16:1-2, 5, 7-8, 9-10, 11

Verse 3

There-fore my heart is glad and my soul re - joic - es, my bod - y, too, a - bides in____ con - fi - dence; be - cause you will not a - ban - don my soul to the neth - er - world, nor will you suf - fer your faith - ful one to un - der - go cor - rup - tion.

Verse 4

You will show me the path to life, a - bound - ing joy____ in your pres - ence, the de - lights at your right____ hand for - ev - er.

Gospel Acclamation: cf. Luke 24:32

Acclamation: (Keyboard/SATB) NO. III

(M.M. ♩ = c. 160)

Al - le - lu - ia, al - le - lu - ia.____

Verse: (Cantor)

Lord____ Jesus, open the Scrip - tures to us;}
{make our hearts burn while you speak to us.

Fourth Sunday of Easter

April 30

Psalm 23:1-3a, 3b-4, 5, 6

Gospel Acclamation: John 10:14

Acclamation: (Keyboard/SATB) NO. IV

Verse: (Cantor)

Fifth Sunday of Easter
May 7

Psalm 33:1-2, 4–5, 18–19

trust - wor - thy. ___ He loves jus - tice and right; of the

to Refrain

kind - ness of the LORD the earth is full. ___

Verse 3

See, the eyes of the LORD are up - on those who fear him,

up - on those who hope for his kind - ness, to de - liv - er them from

to Refrain

death and pre - serve them in spite of fam - ine. ___

Gospel Acclamation: John 14:6

Acclamation: (Keyboard/SATB) NO. I

Al - le - lu - ia, al - le - lu - ia, al - le - lu - ia.

Verse: (Cantor)

to Refrain

I am the way, the truth and the life, says the Lord; / no one comes to the Father, ex - cept through me.

Sixth Sunday of Easter

May 14

Psalm 66:1-3, 4-5, 6-7, 16, 20

Verse 3 (M.M. ♪ = c. 142)

He ___ has changed the sea in - to dry land; through the riv - er they passed on foot; there - fore let us re - joice in him. ___ He rules ___ by ___ his *accel.* might ___ for - ev - er.

Verse 4 (M.M. ♪ = c. 142)

Hear ___ now, all you who fear ___ God, while I de - clare what he has done for me. Bless - ed be ___ God who re - fused me not ___ my prayer or ___ his kind - ness!

Gospel Acclamation: John 14:23

Acclamation: (Keyboard/SATB) NO. II

(M.M. ♩ = c. 130)

Capo 3: A

Al - le - lu - ia, al - le - lu - ia, al - le - lu - ia.

Verse: (Cantor)

Whoever loves me will keep my word, says the Lord, / and my Father will love him / and we will come to him.

The Ascension of the Lord

May 18

The Ascension of the Lord may be celebrated on Thursday May 18 or transferred
to Sunday May 21, depending upon the practice of each province.

Psalm 47:2-3, 6-7, 8-9

(M.M. ♪ = c. 138)

REFRAIN [or: Alleluia]

God mounts his throne to shouts of joy: a blare of trum-pets for the Lord.

Verse 1

All you peo - ples, clap your hands, shout to God with cries of glad - ness. For the LORD, the Most High, the awe - some, is the great king o - ver all the earth.

Verse 2

God mounts his throne a - mid shouts of joy; the LORD, a - mid trum - pet blasts. Sing praise to God, sing praise; sing praise to our king, sing praise.

Verse 3

For ___ king of ___ all the ___ earth is ___ God; sing

hymns of praise. God reigns o - ver the na - tions, ___ God

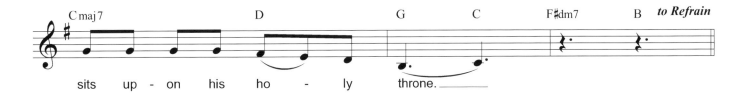

sits up - on his ho - ly throne. ___

Gospel Acclamation: Matthew 28:19a, 20b
Acclamation: (Keyboard/SATB) NO. III

(M.M. ♩ = c. 160)

Capo 3: D/F♯ Em/G A Bm G D A
F/A Gm/B♭ C Dm B♭ F C

Al - le - lu - ia, al - le - lu - ia. ___

Verse: (Cantor)

Em / Gm G / B♭ D / F A / C *to Refrain*

Go and teach all nations, says the Lord;}
{I am with you always, / until the end of the world.

Seventh Sunday of Easter

In those places where the observance of the solemnity of The Ascension of the Lord
has been transferred to this day, Mass and readings of *The Ascension of the Lord* are used.

May 21

Psalm 27:1, 4, 7-8

Gospel Acclamation: cf. John 14:18

Acclamation: (Keyboard/SATB) NO. IV

(M.M. ♩ = c. 116)

Al-le-lu-ia,___ al-le-lu-ia,___ al-le-lu - ia. ia.

Verse: (Cantor)

to Refrain

I will not leave you orphans, / says the Lord. / I will come back to you, / and your}
{hearts will re - joice.

Pentecost Sunday: At the Vigil Mass
(Extended Form)
May 27

Psalm 33:10-11, 12-13, 14-15

to Refrain

down; _____ he sees _____ all _____ man - kind.

Verse 3

From his fixed throne he be - holds all who dwell on the

earth, _____ He who fash - ioned the heart of

to Refrain

each, he who knows _____ all _____ their ___ works.

109

Pentecost Sunday: At the Vigil Mass (Extended Form), cont. (3)

Option 1:

Responsorial Psalm (following second reading)

(M.M. ♩ = c. 74)

Daniel 3:52, 53, 54, 55, 56

to Refrain

praise - wor - thy   and   ex - alt - ed   a - bove   all   for - ev - er."

Verse 4

"Bless-ed   are   you   who look in - to the   depths   from your   throne   up-on   the

to Refrain

cher - u - bim,   praise-wor - thy   and   ex - alt-ed   a - bove   all for - ev - er."

Verse 5

"Bless - ed   are   you   in   the   fir - ma - ment of   heav - en

to Refrain

praise - wor - thy   and   glo - ri - ous   for - ev - er."

Responsorial Psalm (following second reading)

(M.M. ♩ = c. 124)

Psalm 19:8, 9, 10, 11

REFRAIN

Lord, you ___ have the words, ___ Lord, you ___ have the words, ___ you have the words of ev - er - last - ing life. *(Keyboard)*

Verse 1

The law of the LORD is per - fect, re - fresh - ing the soul; ___ the de- cree of the LORD is trust - wor - thy, ___ giv - ing wis - dom to the sim - ple. ___ *to Refrain*

Verse 2

The pre - cepts of the LORD are right, ___ re - joic - ing the heart; ___ the com- mand of the LORD is clear, ___ en - light - en - ing the eye. *to Refrain*

Verse 3

The fear of the LORD is pure, ___ en - dur - ing for - ev - er; ___ the

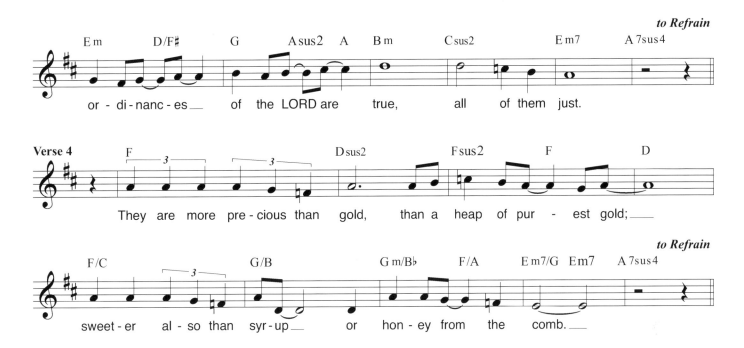

to Refrain

or - di - nanc - es ___ of the LORD are true, all of them just.

Verse 4

They are more pre - cious than gold, than a heap of pur - est gold; ___

to Refrain

sweet - er al - so than syr - up ___ or hon - ey from the comb. ___

Responsorial Psalm (following third reading)

(M.M. ♩ = c. 136)

Psalm 107:2-3, 4-5, 6-7, 8-9

REFRAIN [or: Alleluia]

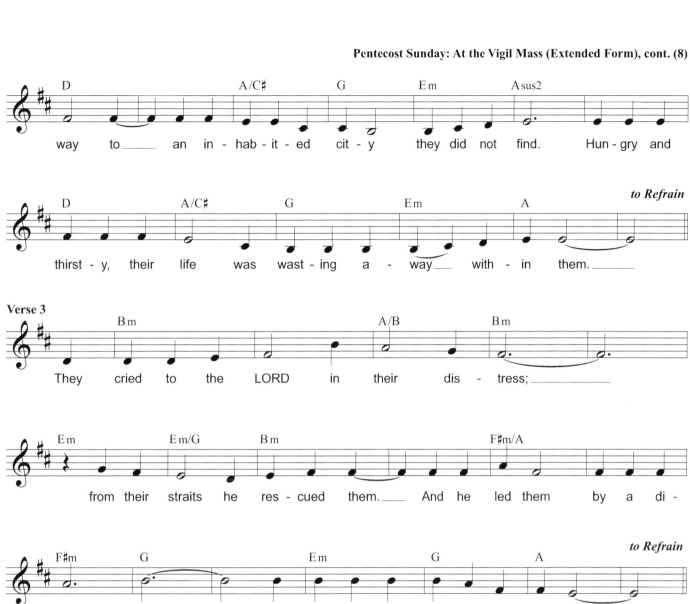

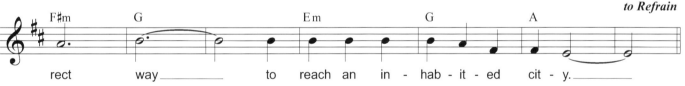

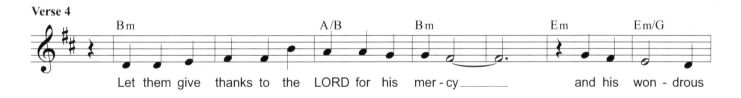

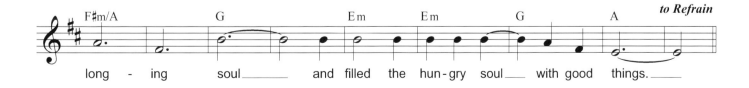

Responsorial Psalm (following fourth reading)

(M.M. ♩ = c. 116)

REFRAIN [or: Alleluia]

Psalm 104:1-2, 24 & 35, 27-28, 29, 30

Verse 3

Crea-tures all look to you to give them food in due

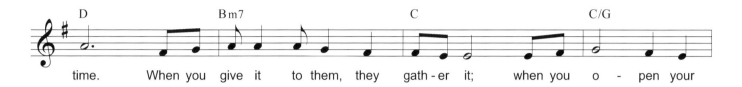

time. When you give it to them, they gath-er it; when you o - pen your

hand, they are filled with good things.

Verse 4

If you take a - way their breath, they per - ish___ and re - turn to their

dust. When you send forth your spir - it,___ they are cre -

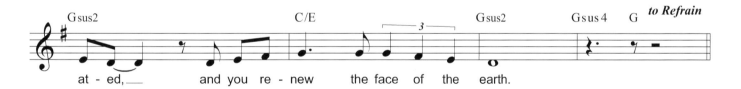

at - ed,___ and you re - new the face of the earth.

Gospel Acclamation:

Acclamation: (Keyboard/SATB) NO. V

(M.M. ♪ = c. 150)

Al - le - lu - ia, al - le - lu - ia. Al - le - lu - ia, al - le - lu - ia.

Verse: (Cantor)

Come, Holy Spirit, fill the hearts of your faithful / and kin - dle in them the fire of your love.

Pentecost Sunday: At the Mass during the Day

May 28

(M.M. ♩ = c. 116)

Psalm 104:1, 24, 29-30, 31, 34

REFRAIN [or: Alleluia]

Lord, send out your Spir - it, and re - new the face of the earth.

Verse 1

Bless the LORD, O my soul! O LORD, my God, you are great in - deed!

How man - i - fold are your works, O LORD! the earth is full of your crea - tures.

Verse 2

If you take a - way their breath, they per - ish and re - turn to their dust. When you send forth your spir - it, they are cre - at - ed, and you re - new the face of the earth.

Verse 3

May the glor - y of the LORD en - dure for -

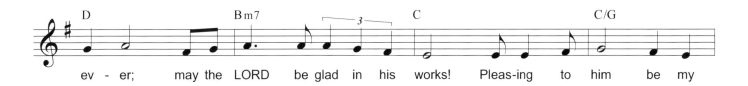

ev - er; may the LORD be glad in his works! Pleas-ing to him be my

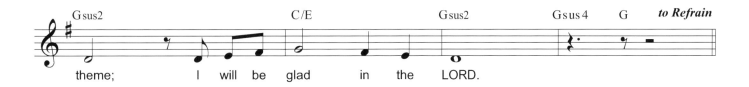

theme; I will be glad in the LORD.

Gospel Acclamation:

Acclamation: (Keyboard/SATB) NO. V

Al - le -lu - ia, al -le -lu - ia. Al - le -lu - ia, al - le -lu - ia.

Verse: (Cantor) *to Refrain*

Come, Holy Spirit, fill the hearts of your faithful / and kin - dle in them the fire of your love.

The Most Holy Trinity

June 4

Through composed octavo Ed. 21021, available at www.ocp.org

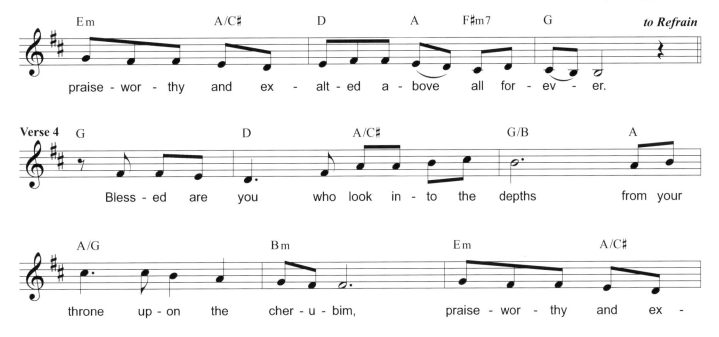

Verse 4

Bless - ed are you who look in - to the depths from your

throne up - on the cher - u - bim, praise - wor - thy and ex -

alt - ed a - bove___ all for - ev - er.

Gospel Acclamation: cf. Revelation 1:8

Acclamation: (Keyboard/SATB) NO. I

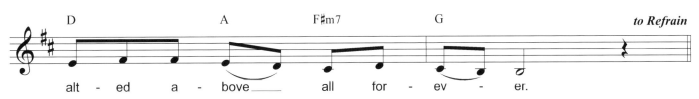

Al - le - lu - ia, al - le - lu - ia, al - le - lu - ia.

Verse: (Cantor)

Glory to the Father, the Son, and the Ho - ly Spirit; / to God who is, who was, / and who is to come.

The Most Holy Body and Blood of Christ (Corpus Christi)

(M.M. ♩ = c. 103)

June 11

Psalm 147:12-13, 14-15, 19-20

Verse 3

He has pro-claimed his word to Ja-cob, his stat-utes and his or-di-nanc-es to

Is - ra - el. He has not done thus for an - y oth - er na - tion; his

or - di - nanc - es he has not made known to them.

Al - le - lu - ia.

Gospel Acclamation: John 6:51

Acclamation: (Keyboard/SATB) NO. II

(M.M. ♩ = c. 130)

Al - le - lu - ia, al - le - lu - ia, al - le - lu - ia.

Verse: (Cantor)

I am the living bread that came down from heaven, says the Lord; / whoever eats this bread will live for - ever.

11th Sunday in Ordinary Time
June 18

(M.M. ♩ = c. 106)

REFRAIN [or: Alleluia]

Psalm 100:1-2, 3, 5

We are his peo - ple, the sheep of his flock.

Verse 1

Sing joy - ful - ly to the LORD, all you lands; serve the LORD with glad - ness; come be - fore him with joy - ful song.

to Refrain

Verse 2

Know that the LORD is God; he made us, his we are; his peo - ple, the flock he tends.

to Refrain

Verse 3

The LORD is good: his kind - ness en-dures for - ev - er, and his faith - ful - ness, to all gen - er - a - tions.

to Refrain

Gospel Acclamation: Mark 1:15

Acclamation: (Keyboard/SATB) NO. I

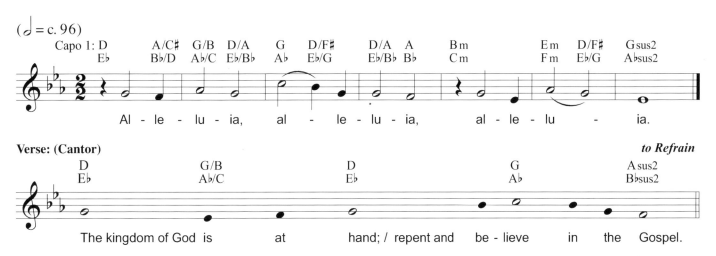

Al - le - lu - ia, al - le - lu - ia, al - le - lu - ia.

Verse: (Cantor) *to Refrain*

The kingdom of God is at hand; / repent and be - lieve in the Gospel.

12th Sunday in Ordinary Time

June 25

Psalm 69:8-10, 14, 17, 33-35

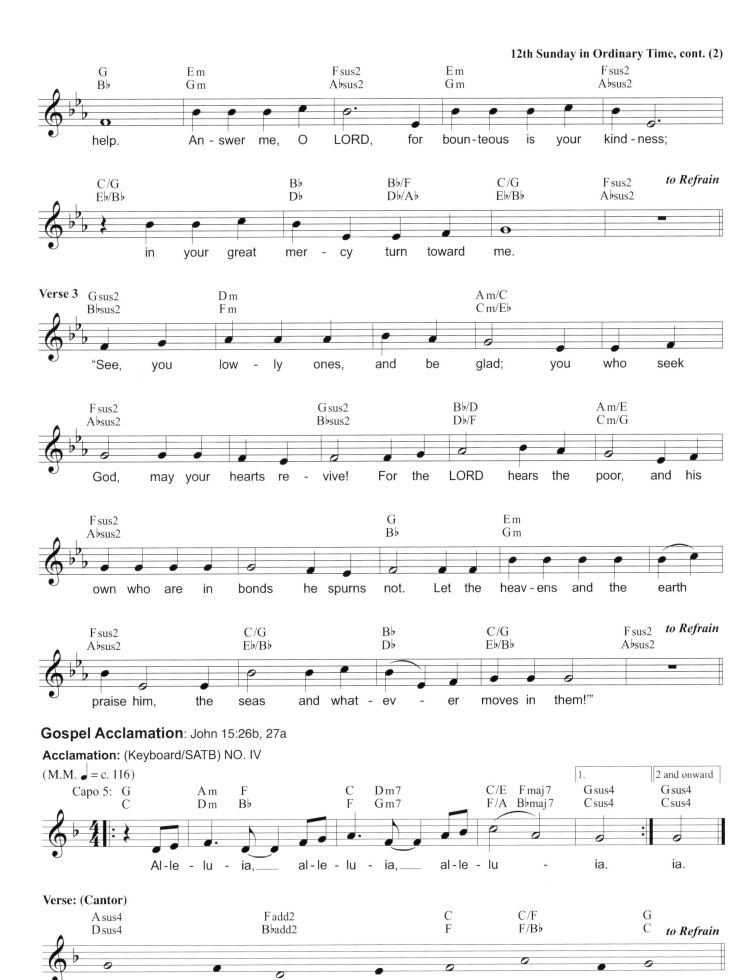

Gospel Acclamation: John 15:26b, 27a

Acclamation: (Keyboard/SATB) NO. IV

13th Sunday in Ordinary Time

July 2

Psalm 89:2-3, 16-17, 18-19

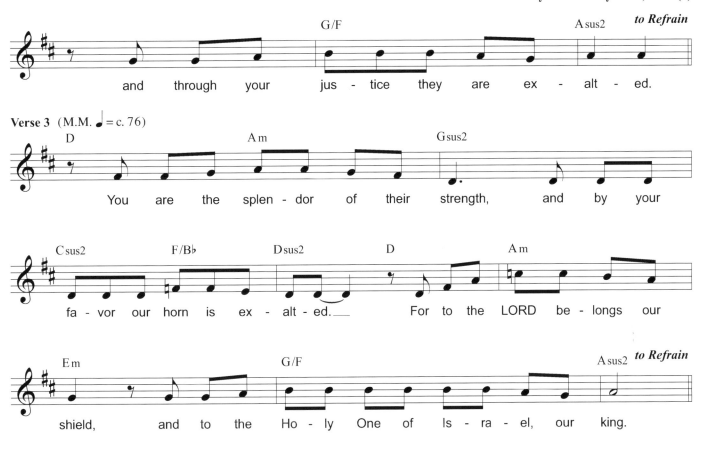

and through your jus - tice they are ex - alt - ed.

Verse 3 (M.M. ♩= c. 76)

You are the splen - dor of their strength, and by your fa - vor our horn is ex - alt - ed.___ For to the LORD be - longs our shield, and to the Ho - ly One of Is - ra - el, our king.

Gospel Acclamation: 1 Peter 2:9

Acclamation: (Keyboard/SATB) NO. IV

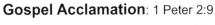
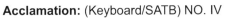
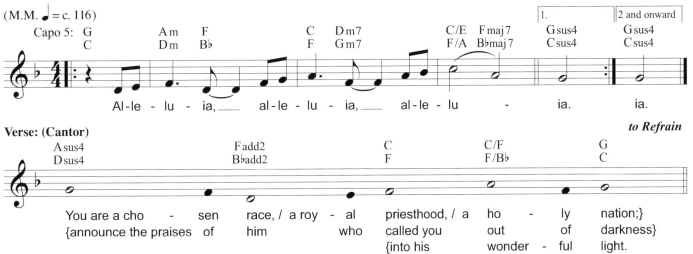

Al - le - lu - ia,___ al - le - lu - ia,___ al - le - lu - ia. ia.

Verse: (Cantor)

You are a cho - sen race, / a roy - al priesthood, / a ho - ly nation;}
{announce the praises of him who called you out of darkness}
{into his wonder - ful light.

14th Sunday in Ordinary Time

July 9

Psalm 145:1-2, 8-9, 10-11, 13-14

Verse 3
Let all your works give you thanks, O LORD, and let your faith-ful ones bless you. Let them dis - course of the glo - ry of your king - dom___ and speak of your might.___

to Refrain

Verse 4
The LORD is faith-ful in all his words and ho - ly in all his___ works.___ The LORD lifts up all who are fall - ing___ and rais - es up all who are bowed down.___

to Refrain

Gospel Acclamation: cf. Matthew 11:25

Acclamation: (Keyboard/SATB) NO. II

(M.M. ♩ = c. 130)

Al - le - lu - ia, al - le - lu - ia, al - le - lu - ia.

Verse: (Cantor)

to Refrain

Blessed are you, Fath - er, Lord of heav - en and earth;}
{you have re - vealed___ to little ones the mysteries of the kingdom.

15th Sunday in Ordinary Time

July 16

(M.M. ♩ = c. 110)

Psalm 65:10, 11, 12-13, 14

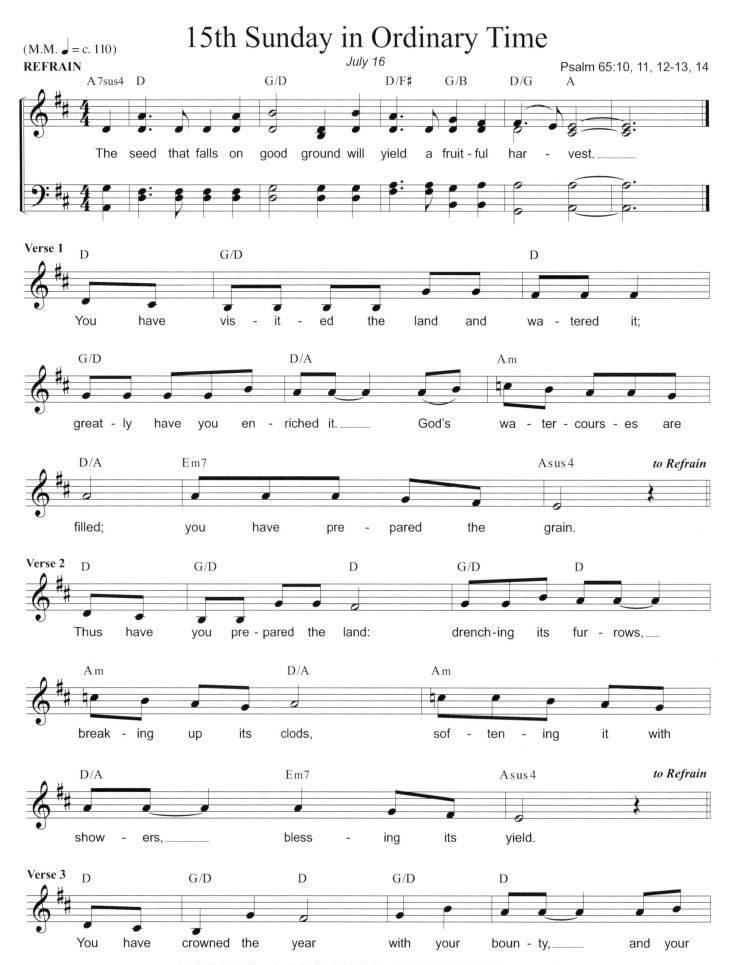

REFRAIN

The seed that falls on good ground will yield a fruit-ful har - vest.

Verse 1
You have vis - it - ed the land and wa - tered it; great - ly have you en - riched it. God's wa - ter - cours - es are filled; you have pre - pared the grain.

Verse 2
Thus have you pre - pared the land: drench-ing its fur - rows, break - ing up its clods, sof - ten - ing it with show - ers, bless - ing its yield.

Verse 3
You have crowned the year with your boun - ty, and your

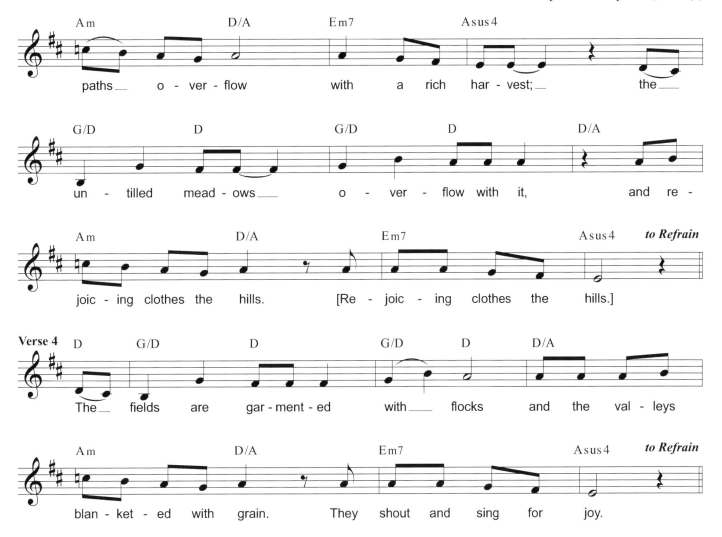

Gospel Acclamation:

Acclamation: (Keyboard/SATB) NO. IV

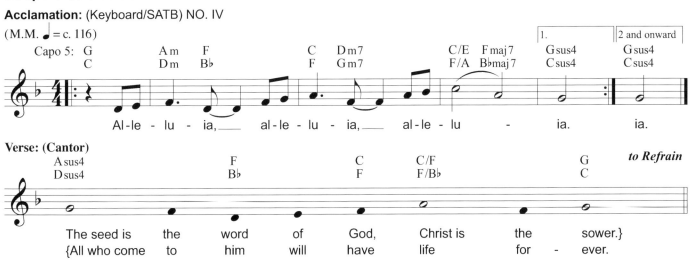

16th Sunday in Ordinary Time

July 23

Psalm 86:5-6, 9-10, 15-16

You, O LORD, are a God mer-ci-ful and gra-cious, slow to an-ger, a-bound-ing in kind-ness and fi-del-i-ty. Turn toward me, and have pit-y on me; give your strength to your ser-vant.

to Refrain

Gospel Acclamation: cf. Matthew 11:25

Acclamation: (Keyboard/SATB) NO. II

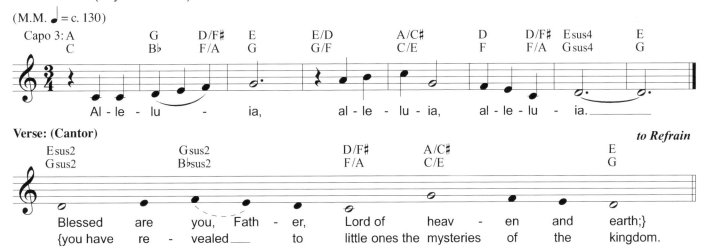

Al-le-lu - ia, al-le-lu-ia, al-le-lu - ia.

Verse: (Cantor)   *to Refrain*

Blessed are you, Fath - er, Lord of heav - en and earth;}
{you have re - vealed___ to little ones the mysteries of the kingdom.

17th Sunday in Ordinary Time

July 30

(Vocals: SAT - Treble Clef
Bass - double melody)

Psalm 119:57, 72, 76-77, 127-128, 129-130

Verse 3

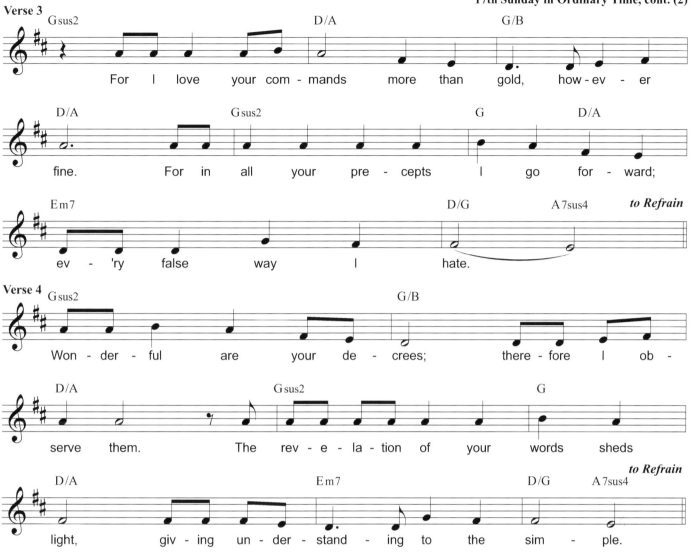

For I love your com - mands more than gold, how - ev - er fine. For in all your pre - cepts I go for - ward; *to Refrain* ev - 'ry false way I hate.

Verse 4

Won - der - ful are your de - crees; there - fore I ob - serve them. The rev - e - la - tion of your words sheds *to Refrain* light, giv - ing un - der - stand - ing to the sim - ple.

Gospel Acclamation: cf. Matthew 11:25

Acclamation: (Keyboard/SATB) NO. II

(M.M. ♩ = c. 130)

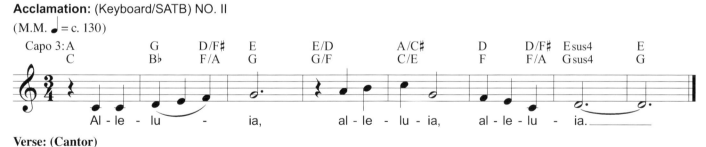

Al - le - lu - ia, al - le - lu - ia, al - le - lu - ia.

Verse: (Cantor)

Blessed are you, Fath - er, Lord of heav - en and earth; / for}
{you have re - vealed___ to little ones the mysteries of the kingdom.

The Transfiguration of the Lord

August 6

jus - tice; _____ and all peo - ples see _____ his glo - ry.

Verse 3

Be - cause you, O LORD, _____ are the Most _____ High _____

o - ver all the earth, ex - alt - ed far a - bove all gods.

Gospel Acclamation: Matthew 17:5c

Acclamation: (Keyboard/SATB) NO. IV

Al - le - lu - ia, _____ al - le - lu - ia, _____ al - le - lu - ia. ia.

Verse: (Cantor)

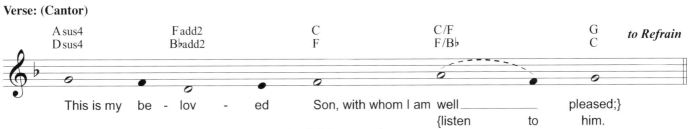

This is my be - lov - ed Son, with whom I am well _____ pleased;}
{listen to him.

19th Sunday in Ordinary Time

August 13

(M.M. ♩ = c. 90)

Psalm 85:9, 10, 11-12, 13-14

REFRAIN

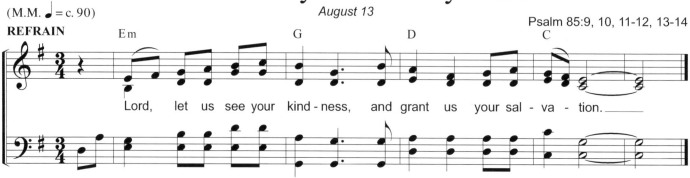

Lord, let us see your kind-ness, and grant us your sal-va-tion.

Verse 1 (M.M. ♩ = c. 76)

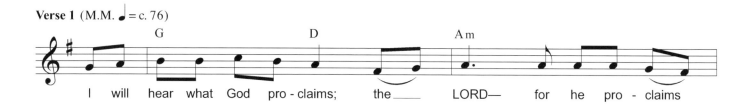

I will hear what God pro-claims; the LORD— for he pro-claims

peace. Near in-deed is his sal-va-tion to

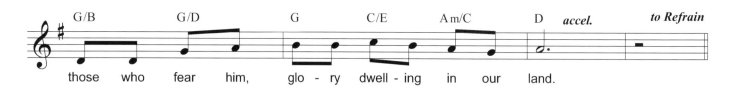

those who fear him, glo-ry dwell-ing in our land.

Verse 2 (M.M. ♩ = c. 76)

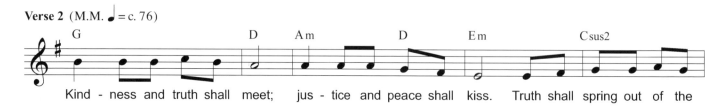

Kind-ness and truth shall meet; jus-tice and peace shall kiss. Truth shall spring out of the

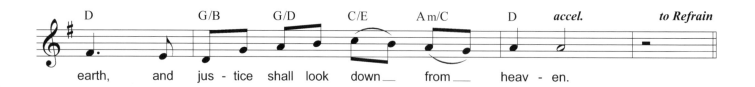

earth, and jus-tice shall look down— from— heav-en.

Verse 3 (M.M. ♩ = c. 76)

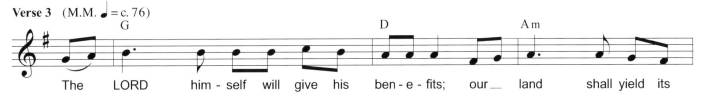

The LORD him-self will give his ben-e-fits; our land shall yield its

in - crease. Jus - tice shall walk be - fore him, and pre -

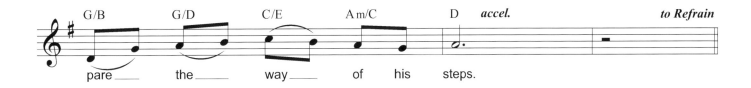

pare the way of his steps.

Gospel Acclamation: cf. Psalm 130:5

Acclamation: (Keyboard/SATB) NO. II

(M.M. ♩ = c. 130)

Al - le - lu - ia, al - le - lu - ia, al - le - lu - ia.

Verse: (Cantor)

I wait for the Lord; / my soul waits for his word.

The Assumption of the Blessed Virgin Mary:
At the Vigil Mass
August 14

Psalm 132:6-7, 9-10, 13-14

Verse 3

For the LORD has cho-sen Zi-on; he pre-fers her for his

dwell-ing. "Zi-on is my rest-ing place for-ev-er; in___

to Refrain

her will I dwell, for___ I pre-fer her."

Gospel Acclamation:

Acclamation: (Keyboard/SATB) NO. III

(M.M. ♩ = c. 160)

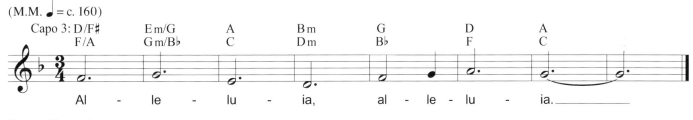

Al - le - lu - ia, al - le - lu - ia.___

Verse: (Cantor)

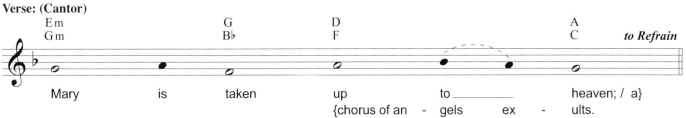

to Refrain

Mary is taken up to___ heaven; / a}
{chorus of an - gels ex - ults.

The Assumption of the Blessed Virgin Mary:
At the Mass during the Day
August 15

Psalm 45:10, 11, 12, 16

(M.M. ♩ = c. 68)

REFRAIN

The queen stands at your right hand, ar-rayed in gold.

Verse 1

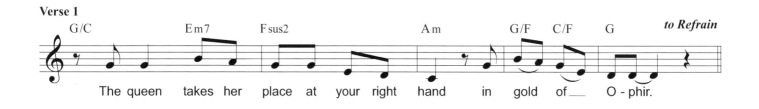

The queen takes her place at your right hand in gold of __ O - phir.

Verse 2

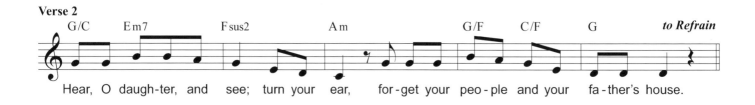

Hear, O daugh-ter, and see; turn your ear, for-get your peo-ple and your fa-ther's house.

Verse 3

So shall the king de-sire __ your beau-ty; __ for he __ is your lord.

Verse 4

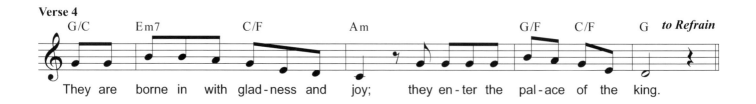

They are borne in with glad-ness and joy; they en-ter the pal-ace of the king.

Gospel Acclamation:

Acclamation: (Keyboard/SATB) NO. III

(M.M. ♩ = c. 160)

Al - le - lu - ia, al - le - lu - ia._____

Verse: (Cantor)

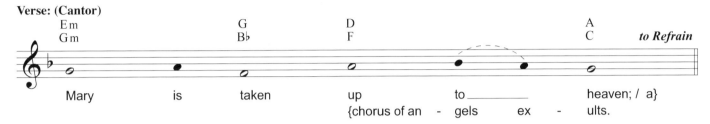

Mary   is   taken   up   to _____   heaven; / a}
{chorus of an - gels ex - ults.

20th Sunday in Ordinary Time

August 20

Psalm 67:2-3, 5, 6, 8

rule __ the peo - ples in eq - ui - ty; __ the na - tions __ on the earth you guide. __

to Refrain

Verse 3

May the peo - ples praise you, O God;

may all __ the peo - ples praise you! __

May __ God bless us, and may all the ends of the earth __

to Refrain

fear him! __

Gospel Acclamation: cf. Matthew 4:23

Acclamation: (Keyboard/SATB) NO. I

Al - le - lu - ia, al - le - lu - ia, al - le - lu - ia.

Verse: (Cantor)

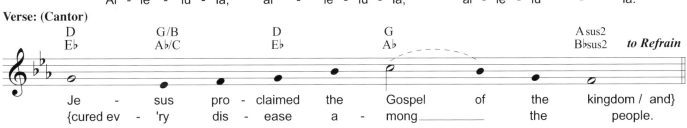

Je - sus pro - claimed the Gospel of the kingdom / and}
{cured ev - 'ry dis - ease a - mong __ the people.

to Refrain

21st Sunday in Ordinary Time

August 27

Psalm 138:1-2, 2-3, 6, 8

Verse 3

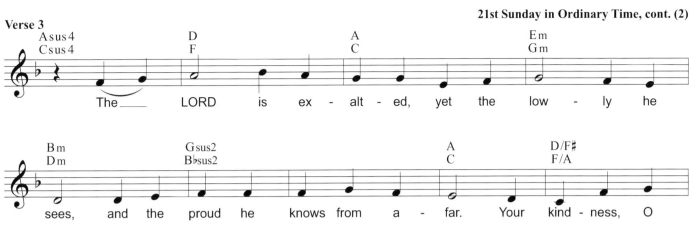

The LORD is ex - alt - ed, yet the low - ly he

sees, and the proud he knows from a - far. Your kind - ness, O

LORD, en - dures for - ev - er; for - sake not the work of your hands.

Gospel Acclamation: Matthew 16:18

Acclamation: (Keyboard/SATB) NO. III

Al - le - lu - ia, al - le - lu - ia.

Verse: (Cantor)

You are Peter and upon this rock I will build my Church / and the}
{gates of the netherworld shall not pre - vail a - gainst it.

22nd Sunday in Ordinary Time

September 3

Psalm 63:2, 3-4, 5-6, 8-9

call up-on your name. As with the rich-es of a ban-quet shall my soul be

sat - is - fied, and with ex - ult - ant lips my mouth shall praise you.

to Refrain

Verse 4

You ___ are my help,

and in the sha - dow ___ of your wings I shout for joy.

My soul clings fast to you; your right ___ hand up -

to Refrain

holds me. ___

Gospel Acclamation: Ephesians 1:17-18
Acclamation: (Keyboard/SATB) NO. II

(M.M. ♩ = c. 130)

Al - le - lu - ia, al - le - lu - ia, al - le - lu - ia.

to Refrain

Verse: (Cantor)

May the Father of our Lord Je - sus Christ en - lighten the eyes of our hearts,}
{that we may know what is the hope that be - longs ___ to ___ our call.

23rd Sunday in Ordinary Time
September 10

Psalm 95:1-2, 6-7, 8-9

Verse 3

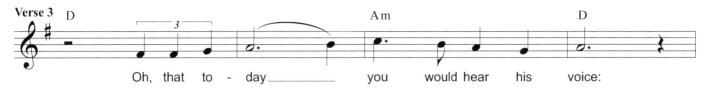

Oh, that to-day _____ you would hear his voice:

"Hard-en not your hearts as at Mer-i-bah, as in the day of Mas-sah___ in the

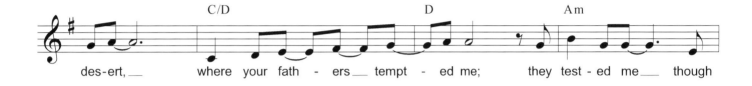

des-ert, ___ where your fath - ers___ tempt - ed me; they test-ed me___ though

they had___ seen___ my___ works." ___

Gospel Acclamation: 2 Corinthians 5:19

Acclamation: (Keyboard/SATB) NO. IV

(M.M. ♩ = c. 116)

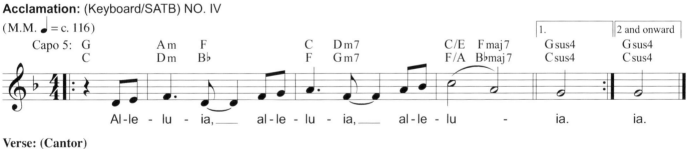

Al-le-lu - ia, ___ al-le-lu - ia, ___ al-le-lu - ia. ia.

Verse: (Cantor)

God was re - con - ciling the world to him - self in Christ / and en –}
{trusting to us the message of reconcil - i - ation.

24th Sunday in Ordinary Time

September 17

Psalm 103:1-2, 3-4, 9-10, 11-12

Gospel Acclamation: John 13:34

Acclamation: (Keyboard/SATB) NO. I

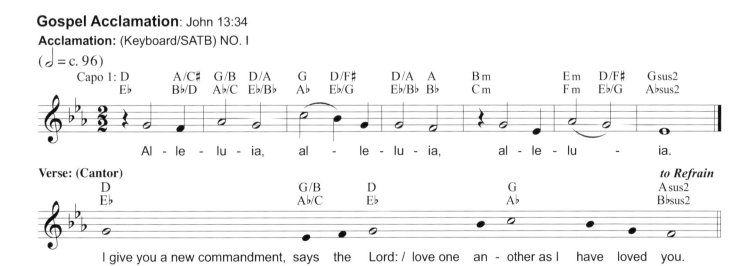

25th Sunday in Ordinary Time
September 24

Verse 3

The LORD is just in all his ways and__ ho - ly in all his works. The LORD is near to all who call up - on him, to all who

to Refrain

call up - on him in truth.__

Gospel Acclamation: Acts of the Apostles 16:14b

Acclamation: (Keyboard/SATB) NO. IV

(M.M. ♩ = c. 116)

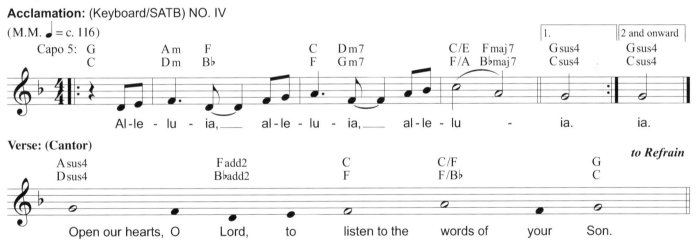

Al - le - lu - ia,__ al - le - lu - ia,__ al - le - lu - ia. ia.

Verse: (Cantor)

to Refrain

Open our hearts, O Lord, to listen to the words of your Son.

26th Sunday in Ordinary Time

October 1

Psalm 25:4-5, 6-7, 8-9

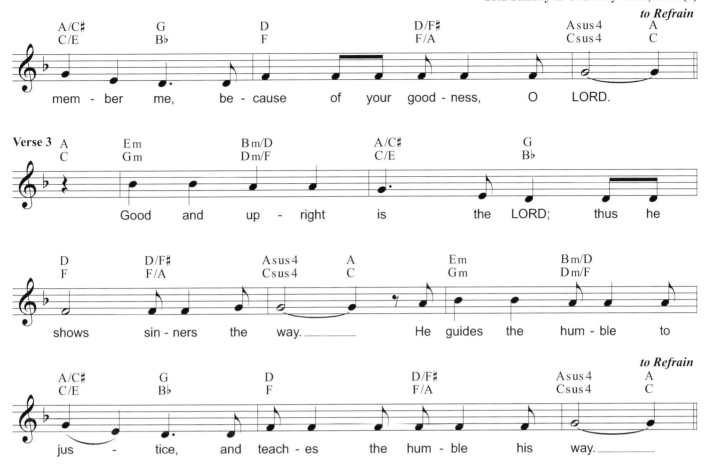

to Refrain

| A/C♯ | G | D | D/F♯ | Asus4 | A |
| C/E | B♭ | F | F/A | Csus4 | C |

mem - ber me, be - cause of your good - ness, O LORD.

Verse 3

| A | Em | Bm/D | A/C♯ | G |
| C | Gm | Dm/F | C/E | B♭ |

Good and up - right is the LORD; thus he

| D | D/F♯ | Asus4 A | Em | Bm/D |
| F | F/A | Csus4 C | Gm | Dm/F |

shows sin - ners the way.____ He guides the hum - ble to

to Refrain

| A/C♯ | G | D | D/F♯ | Asus4 | A |
| C/E | B♭ | F | F/A | Csus4 | C |

jus - tice, and teach - es the hum - ble his way.____

Gospel Acclamation: John 10:27

Acclamation: (Keyboard/SATB) NO. IV

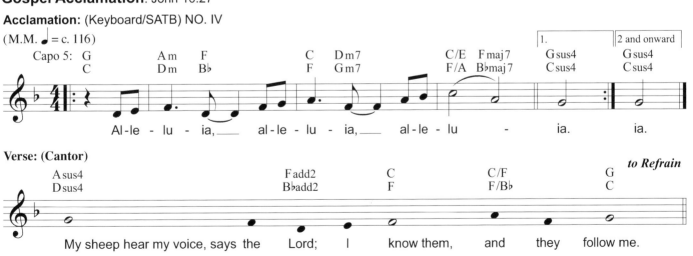

(M.M. ♩ = c. 116)

Capo 5:

| G | Am F | C Dm7 | C/E Fmaj7 | [1.] Gsus4 | [2 and onward] Gsus4 |
| | C Dm B♭ | F Gm7 | F/A B♭maj7 | Csus4 | Csus4 |

Al -le - lu - ia,____ al -le - lu - ia,____ al -le - lu - ia. ia.

Verse: (Cantor)

to Refrain

| Asus4 | Fadd2 | C | C/F | G |
| Dsus4 | B♭add2 | F | F/B♭ | C |

My sheep hear my voice, says the Lord; I know them, and they follow me.

27th Sunday in Ordinary Time

October 8

Psalm 80:9, 12, 13-14, 15-16, 19-20

Verse 3

Once a-gain, O LORD of hosts, look down from heav - en, and see; take care of this vine, and pro - tect___ what your right___ hand has plant-ed, the son of man whom you your - self made___ strong.

to Refrain

Verse 4

Then we will no more with-draw from you; give us new life, and we will call up - on your name. O LORD, God of hosts, re - store us;___ if your face shine up - on us, then we shall be saved.

to Refrain

Gospel Acclamation: cf. John 15:16

Acclamation: (Keyboard/SATB) NO. I

($\downarrow$ = c. 96)

Capo 1: D   A/C♯   G/B   D/A   G   D/F♯   D/A   A   Bm   Em   D/F♯   Gsus2
E♭   B♭/D   A♭/C   E♭/B♭   A♭   E♭/G   E♭/B♭   B♭   Cm   Fm   E♭/G   A♭sus2

Al - le - lu - ia, al - le - lu - ia, al - le - lu - ia.

Verse: (Cantor)   *to Refrain*

D   G/B   D   G   Asus2
E♭   A♭/C   E♭   A♭   B♭sus2

I have chosen you from the world, says the Lord, / to go and bear fruit that will re - main.

28th Sunday in Ordinary Time

October 15

(M.M. ♩ = c. 108)

Psalm 23:1-3a, 3b-4, 5, 6

| A | F#m7 | G | Asus4 | A | *to Refrain* |
| C | Am7 | Bb | Csus4 | C | |

side with your rod and your staff___ that give me cour-age.

Verse 3

| Em | Bm/D | Cmaj7 | Bm |
| Gm | Dm/F | Ebmaj7 | Dm |

You spread the ta - ble be - fore me in the sight of my foes; you a -

| D | A | Em7 | Em/G |
| F | C | Gm7 | Gm/Bb |

noint my___ head with oil; my___ cup o - ver -

| Asus4 | A | *to Refrain* | **Verse 4** Em | Bm/D |
| Csus4 | C | | Gm | Dm/F |

flows. On - ly good - ness and kind - ness fol - low me

| Cmaj7 | Bm | D | A |
| Ebmaj7 | Dm | F | C |

all the days of my life; and I shall dwell in the house of the

| Em7 | G | Asus4 | A | *to Refrain* |
| Gm7 | Bb | Csus4 | C | |

LORD for years to come.

Gospel Acclamation: Ephesians 1:17-18

Acclamation: (Keyboard/SATB) NO. II

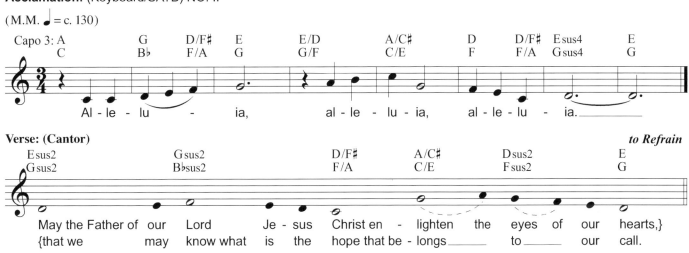

(M.M. ♩ = c. 130)

| Capo 3: A | G | D/F# | E | E/D | A/C# | D | D/F# | Esus4 | E |
| C | Bb | F/A | G | G/F | C/E | F | F/A | Gsus4 | G |

Al - le - lu - ia, al - le - lu - ia, al - le - lu - ia.___

Verse: (Cantor)   *to Refrain*

| Esus2 | Gsus2 | D/F# | A/C# | Dsus2 | E |
| Gsus2 | Bbsus2 | F/A | C/E | Fsus2 | G |

May the Father of our Lord Je - sus Christ en - lighten the eyes of our hearts,}
{that we may know what is the hope that be - longs___ to___ our call.

29th Sunday in Ordinary Time

October 22

Psalm 96:1, 3, 4-5, 7-8, 9-10

(M.M. ♩ = c. 140)

Give the Lord glo-ry and hon-or. Give the Lord glo-ry and hon - or.

Verse 1

Sing to the LORD a new____ song; sing to the LORD, all you lands. Tell his glo-ry a - mong____ the na - tions;____ a - mong all peo - ples, his won - drous deeds.

Verse 2

For great is the LORD and high - ly to be praised; awe - some is he, be - yond all gods. For all the gods of the na - tions are things____ of nought, but the LORD made the heav - ens.____

Verse 3

Give to the LORD, you fam - i - lies of na - tions, give to the LORD glo - ry and praise; ___ give to the LORD the glo - ry due ___ his name! ___ Bring

to Refrain **Verse 4**

gifts, and en - ter his courts. ___ Wor - ship the LORD in ho - ly at - tire.

Trem - ble be - fore him, all the earth; say a - mong the na - tions: The

LORD ___ is king, he gov - erns the peo - ples with e - qui - ty. ___ A *to Refrain*

Gospel Acclamation: Philippians 2:15d, 16a

Acclamation: (Keyboard/SATB) NO. I

Al - le - lu - ia, al - le - lu - ia, al - le - lu - ia.

Verse: (Cantor) *to Refrain*

Shine like lights in the world as you hold on to the word of life.

30th Sunday in Ordinary Time

October 29

Psalm 18:2-3, 3-4, 47, 51

Gospel Acclamation: John 14:23

Acclamation: (Keyboard/SATB) NO. II

All Saints

November 1

(M.M. ♩ = c. 94)

Psalm 24:1bc-2, 3-4ab, 5-6

REFRAIN

Lord, this is the peo-ple that longs to see your face.

Lord, this is the peo-ple that longs to see your face.____

Verse 1

The LORD's are the earth and its full-ness; the world and those who dwell in it. For he found-ed it up-on the seas and___ es-tab-lished it up-on___ the riv-ers.___

to Refrain

Verse 2

Who can as-cend the moun-tain of the LORD? or who may stand in his

ho-ly place? One whose hands are sin-less, whose heart is clean, who de-

to Refrain Verse 3

sires not what is vain._____ He shall re-ceive a bless-ing from the

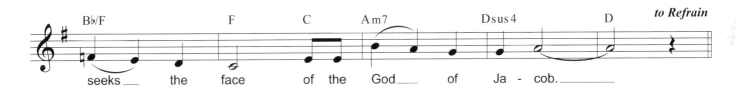

LORD, a re-ward from God his sav-ior. Such is the race that seeks him, that

to Refrain

seeks___ the face of the God___ of Ja - cob._____

Gospel Acclamation: Matthew 11:28

Acclamation: (Keyboard/SATB) NO. I

(M.M. ♩ = c. 96)

Al - le - lu - ia, al - le - lu - ia, al - le - lu - ia.

Verse: (Cantor)   *to Refrain*

Come to me, all you who labor and are burdened, / and I will give you rest, says the Lord.

31st Sunday in Ordinary Time

November 5

Verse 3

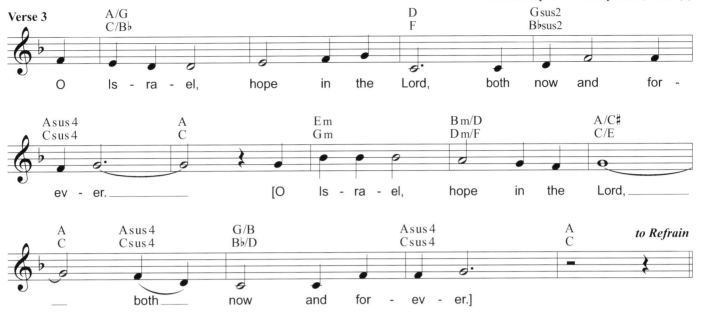

O Is - ra - el, hope in the Lord, both now and for - ev - er._____ [O Is - ra - el, hope in the Lord,_____ both_____ now and for - ev - er.]

to Refrain

Gospel Acclamation: Matthew 23:9b, 10b

Acclamation: (Keyboard/SATB) NO. IV

(M.M. ♩ = c. 116)

Al - le - lu - ia,____ al - le - lu - ia,____ al - le - lu - ia. ia.

Verse: (Cantor)

to Refrain

You have but one Father in heaven / and one master, the Christ.

32nd Sunday in Ordinary Time

November 12

Psalm 63:2, 3-4, 5-6, 7-8

call up-on your name. As with the rich-es of a ban-quet shall my soul be sat - is - fied, and with ex-ult-ant lips my mouth shall praise you.

to Refrain

Verse 4

I will re-mem-ber you up-on my couch, and through the night-watch-es I will med-i-tate on you: you are my help, and in the shad - ow of your wings I shout for joy.

to Refrain

Gospel Acclamation: Matthew 24:42a, 44

Acclamation: (Keyboard/SATB) NO. I

Al-le-lu-ia, al-le-lu-ia, al-le-lu - ia.

Verse: (Cantor)

to Refrain

Stay awake and be ready! / For you do _____ not know on what] {day your Lord _____ will come.

33rd Sunday in Ordinary Time

November 19

Psalm 128:1-2, 3, 4-5

of Je - ru - sa - lem   all the days___ of your life.

Gospel Acclamation: John 15:4a, 5b

Acclamation: (Keyboard/SATB) NO. IV

Al-le - lu - ia,___ al-le-lu - ia,___ al-le-lu - ia.   ia.

Verse: (Cantor)

to Refrain

Remain in me   as   I remain   in   you,   says   the   Lord. / Who –
{ever   re - mains   in   me   bears   much   fruit.

Thanksgiving Day

November 23

(M.M. ♩ = c. 78)

Psalm 113:1-2, 3-4, 5-6, 7-8

For alternate **Responsorial Psalms**, see *Lectionary for the Mass, Second Typical Edition* #945.

Verse 3: Who is like the LORD, our God, who is en - throned on high and looks up - on the heav - ens and the earth be - low?

Verse 4: He rais - es up the low - ly from the dust; from the dung - hill he lifts up the poor to seat them with princ - es, with the princ - es of his own peo - ple.

Gospel Acclamation: 1 Thessalonians 5:18

Acclamation: (Keyboard/SATB) NO. II

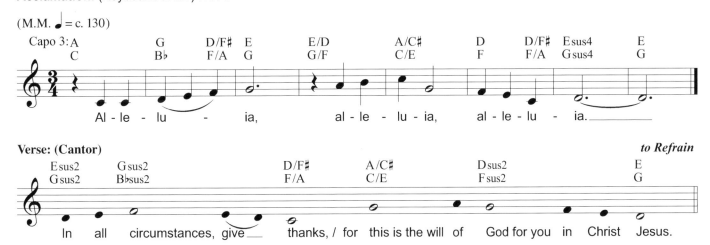

Al - le - lu - ia, al - le - lu - ia, al - le - lu - ia.

Verse: (Cantor) *to Refrain*

In all circumstances, give thanks, / for this is the will of God for you in Christ Jesus.

For alternate **Gospel Acclamation Verses**, see *Lectionary for the Mass, Second Typical Edition* #946.

Our Lord Jesus Christ, King of the Universe

(M.M. ♩ = c. 114)

November 26

Psalm 23:1-2, 2-3, 5, 6

noint my head with oil;_____ my

cup____ o - ver - flows._____

Verse 4

On - ly good-ness and kind - ness fol - low me all the days of my

life; and I shall dwell in the house of the LORD_____ for

years____ to come._____

Gospel Acclamation: Mark 11:9, 10

Acclamation: (Keyboard/SATB) NO. V

(M.M. ♪ = c. 150)

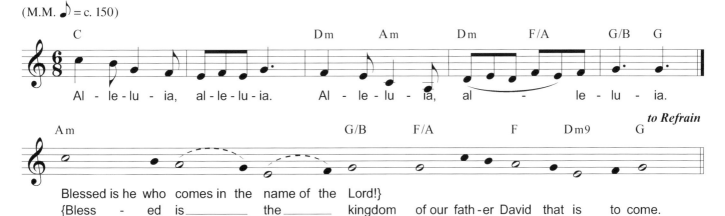

Al - le - lu - ia, al - le - lu - ia. Al - le - lu - ia, al - le - lu - ia.

Blessed is he who comes in the name of the Lord!}
{Bless - ed is____ the____ kingdom of our fath-er David that is to come.

Rite of Entrance into the Order of Catechumens

(M.M. ♪ = c. 132)

Psalm 33:4-5, 12-13, 18-19, 20 & 22

REFRAIN

Alternate ending

Bless-ed the peo-ple the Lord has chos-en, the Lord has chos-en to be his own.

Optional Interlude before Verse 3 & after final Refrain

Verse 1

For up-right __ is the word of the LORD, and all his works are trust-wor-thy. __

He loves jus-tice and right; of the kind-ness of the LORD the earth is full.

to Refrain

Verse 2

Bless-ed the na-tion whose God is the LORD, the peo-ple he has

cho-sen for his own in-her-it-ance. From heav-en the LORD looks

down; __ he sees __ all __ man-kind.

to Refrain

Alternate response: "Lord, let your mercy be on us, as we place our trust in you."

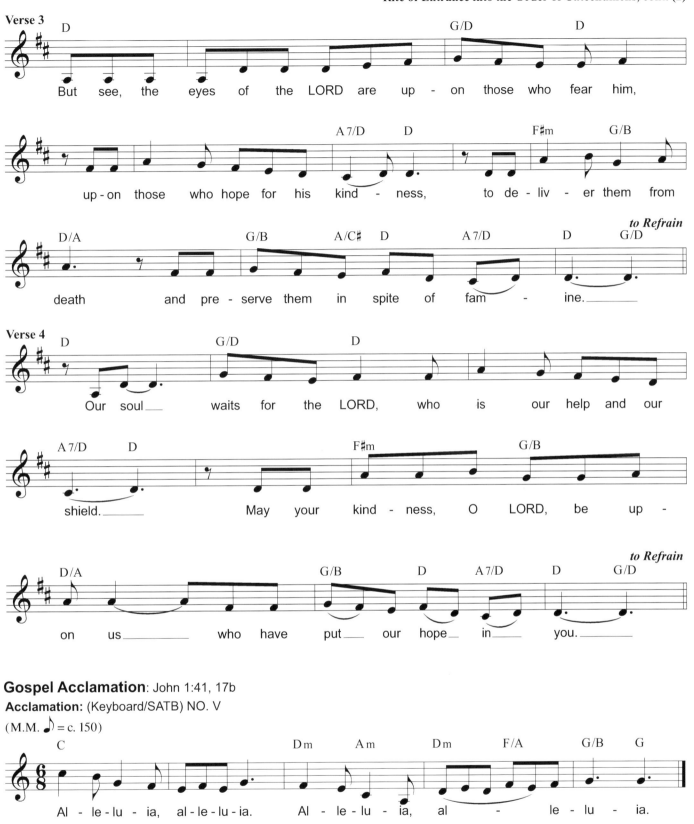

Verse 3

But see, the eyes of the LORD are up - on those who fear him, up - on those who hope for his kind - ness, to de - liv - er them from death and pre - serve them in spite of fam - ine.

to Refrain

Verse 4

Our soul waits for the LORD, who is our help and our shield. May your kind - ness, O LORD, be up - on us who have put our hope in you.

to Refrain

Gospel Acclamation: John 1:41, 17b

Acclamation: (Keyboard/SATB) NO. V

(M.M. ♪ = c. 150)

Al - le - lu - ia, al - le - lu - ia. Al - le - lu - ia, al - le - lu - ia.

to Refrain

We have found the Mes - si - ah: Je - sus Christ, through whom came truth and grace.

Selected Psalm for Weddings

Alternate Response: "See how the Lord blesses those who fear him."

For alternate **Responsorial Psalms** for weddings, see *Lectionary for the Mass, Second Typical Edition* #803.

bless you from ____ Zi - on: ____ may you see the pros - per - i - ty

to Refrain

of Je - ru - sa - lem all the days ____ of your life.

Selected Psalm for Funerals

Psalm 103:8 & 10, 13-14, 15-16, 17-18

Alternate response: "The salvation of the just comes from the Lord."

For alternate **Responsorial Psalms** for funerals, see *Lectionary for the Mass, Second Typical Edition* #1013.

Verse 3

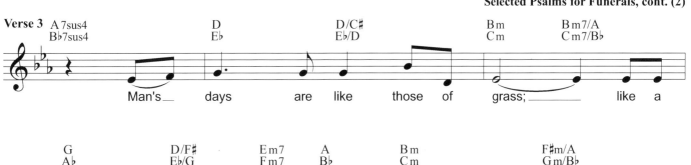

Man's days are like those of grass; like a

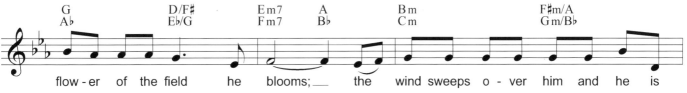

flow-er of the field he blooms; the wind sweeps o-ver him and he is

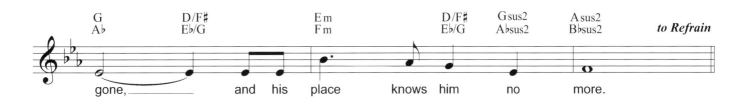

to Refrain

gone, and his place knows him no more.

Verse 4

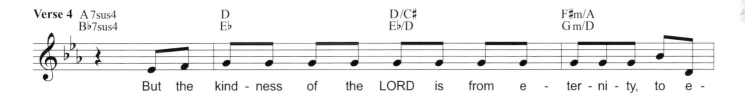

But the kind-ness of the LORD is from e-ter-ni-ty, to e-

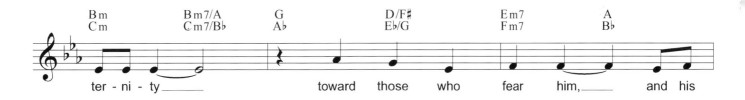

ter-ni-ty toward those who fear him, and his

jus-tice toward chil-dren's chil-dren a-mong those who keep his

to Refrain

cov-e-nant and re-mem-ber to ful-fill his pre-cepts.

Selected Common (Seasonal) Psalm for Ordinary Time

(M.M. ♩ = c. 72)

Psalm 27:1, 4, 13-14

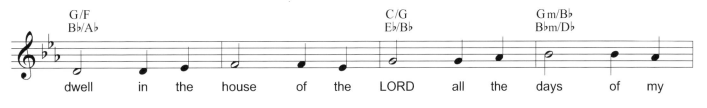

dwell in the house of the LORD all the days of my

life. that I may gaze on the love - li - ness_____ of the

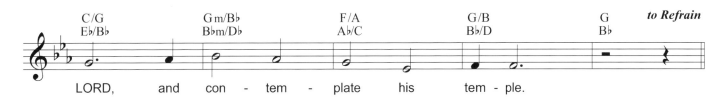

LORD, and con - tem - plate his tem - ple.

Verse 3

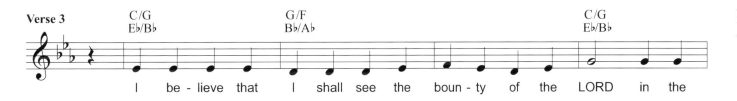

I be - lieve that I shall see the boun - ty of the LORD in the

land of the liv - ing. Wait for the LORD with cour - age;_____

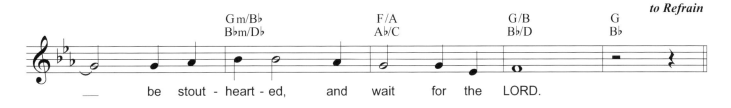

_____ be stout - heart - ed, and wait for the LORD.

Made in the USA
Columbia, SC
31 October 2022

70262535R00102